New York Times bestselling author

TERESA GIUDICE

**With Heather Maclean
Photographs by Sheri Giblin**

Fabulicious!

FAST & FIT

New York Times **bestselling author**

TERESA GIUDICE

With Heather Maclean
Photographs by Sheri Giblin

Fabulicious!

FAST & FIT

Teresa's **Low-Fat,**
Super-Easy Italian Recipes

RUNNING PRESS
PHILADELPHIA · LONDON

ISBN 978-0-7624-4544-8
Library of Congress Control Number: 2012930473

E-book ISBN 978-0-7624-4562-2

9   8   7   6   5   4   3
Digit on the right indicates the number of this printing

Cover and interior design by Frances J. Soo Ping Chow
Edited by Jennifer Kasius
Food Styling by Erin Quon
Prop Styling by Matthew Gleason
Typography: Affair, Archer, Baskerville, Bodega Sans, La Portentia,
Neutra, Samantha, Sweet Rosie, and Swingdancer

Running Press Book Publishers
2300 Chestnut Street
Philadelphia, PA 19103-4371

Visit us on the web!
www.runningpresscooks.com

Dedication

I dedicate this book to my mom.

You are my best friend.
You have inspired me in more ways than you will ever know.

Sei bella dentro e fuori.

ACKNOWLEDGMENTS

First I want to thank my family—my wonderful husband, Joe, my beautiful daughters Gia, Gabriella, Milania, and Audriana, and my parents Antonia and Giacinto Gorga. You mean everything to me. You inspire me, you make me happy, you give me more love than anyone deserves. Thank you too to my extended family, and all of my friends and fans—your support means the world to me.

A million hugs to Heather Maclean for taking this journey with me. We started out as writing partners and ended up as friends. Thank you to my agent Susan Ginsburg and all the amazing people at Writers House for taking a chance on me, encouraging me, and being so wonderful.

And a giant thank you to: the entire team at Running Press, especially Chris Navratil, Jennifer Kasius, Craig Herman, and Frances Soo Ping Chow for your incredible talent; to Rick Rodgers for your culinary genius; to Sheri Giblin for your gifted eye; and to my beautiful friends Priscilla DiStasio and Edyta Keska for joining me in the photos.

I love love love you all! xx

Contents

Chapter 4

Soup It Up—Hot & Cold Comfort Food

Chapter 5

Switch It Up—Low-Fat Italian Classics

Chapter 6

Step It Up—Gourmet Entrées

Chapter 7

Grill It Up—Sizzling Selections

Chapter 8

Veg It Up—Vegetarian Meals & Side Dishes

Chapter 9

Whip It Up—Extra Fast Food

Chapter 10

Spice It Up—Some Like It HOT

Chapter 11

Sex It Up—Romantic Meals

Chapter 12

Sweeten It Up—Guilt-Free Desserts

Last Word

Lots of F-Words

I've always been partial to the letters "T" and "G" since they've been my initials my whole life, first when I was Teresa Gorga and now as Teresa Giudice. And I love the letter "A" as an ending for any girl's name, as you can tell from mine, my mama Antonia's, and all four of my girls: Gia, Gabriella, Milania, and Audriana.

But in the last year, I've gotten a new favorite letter: "F." If you watched me in the first season of *The Real Housewives of New Jersey*, you might think you know why "F" is my favorite letter, but you'd be wrong. It's not that F-word. (Please, I'm a lady!) It's not for my Infamous Table Flip (I have only ever done that once in my life, and will never do it again, trust me!). "F" is a huge part of my life now for more than one reason, actually.

I taught my girls to say "Faaaabulousss!" from the time they could talk, and I really do take that as one of my life philosophies. No matter where I lived, with my parents in Paterson, New Jersey, or in my beautiful house with my hubby; no matter what my job was, buyer for Macy's or stay-at-home mom; no matter how much money I did or didn't have, I always truly believed I was Fabulous.

"Fabulous" is the word I wanted people to think of when they met me. Not just for my clothes or my hair, but for my attitude and my smile. Fabulous is definitely a state of mind. Not every day will be Fabulous. You won't always have Fabulous luck. But you can always decide to BE Fabulous. (And don't let anyone tell you different—Fabulous is free!)

I don't remember when I started using the word "Fabulicious," but it was way before I was ever on Bravo. As most of you know, I was conceived in Italy and born in America. I grew up speaking Italian, and like a lot of bilingual kids, I've made up my own words my whole life. Some of them are a little insane and hard to figure out where they came from (like "chuckalina" . . . and that's all we'll say on that subject!), but "Fabulicious" is easy: it came from my favorite way to be, "Fabulous," plus my favorite way to cook and eat: "Delicious."

Before I was on TV, I opened a little online boutique called Fabulicious, which is now also the name of my website. And I was so excited to get to name my second *New York Times* bestselling book *Fabulicious!: Teresa's Italian Family Cookbook* as well. Finally, I got my favorite word out to the masses! Hopefully you are all embracing your fabulous selves and cooking delicious meals with your family.

"Family" is without question the most important F-word in my life (and if you've ever had a family feud in yours, you know "f-word" can be used in multiple ways here . . .). I am so blessed to have such a wonderful family. I cannot say enough about my parents and how thankful I am for the upbringing they gave me. They taught me more than just how to cook, they taught me how to live, how to love, and most importantly, how to never give up. My amazing husband, Joe, has been my best friend and my rock since we were kids. My gorgeous, gorgeous girls are my world. I truly love my entire family: my brother, my niece and nephews, all of my in-laws, my aunt and cousins, and my extended family in Italy and Belgium.

Another F-word that had a couple different meanings for me this last year was "Friends." I have so many amazing friends—the most amazing of which are happily anonymous, staying far, far from my public life. They are my refuge. Like all good friends, they always have my back, they are there for me in any circumstance, and they make me smile. And, as I've been traveling the country meeting people at book signings and appearances and getting to know my fans online, I've found that they are also the best of both worlds—friends and family. I love, love, love you all!

The letter "F" was obviously also a big hit with my publishers, as they loved the new title: *Fabulicious! Fast & Fit.*

It was just so perfect because while fabulous and delicious is my specialty, I don't want anyone to forget that food, especially authentic Italian food made at home with fresh ingredients and lots of love, can also be made quickly and complement (or even jumpstart!) your healthy lifestyle.

I promise you both things in this cookbook: The recipes are fast and will help you stay fit.

FAST

My mother will tell you I was born kicking. I've always been in a hurry. My father used to say I had *pepe in piedi* or pepper in my feet (I guess that's like a pep in your step?). I couldn't sit still. I still can't. Once I started working, got married, had kids, of course it only got worse. There just isn't enough time in the day to do everything I want to do!

I love to cook and I have no problem spending hours and hours in the kitchen. I love complicated dishes with lots of ingredients . . . sometimes. But most days, I just don't have time to prep a two-hour dinner. And I'm sure you don't either. That's why I included only my "fast" recipes in this book.

Every recipe here can go from Start to Stove in less than thirty minutes. There aren't a lot of steps, you don't need a million pots, and most everything can be made with a few pantry staples (I'll give you a complete list in the next chapter). Because you need to make sure meat is cooked all the way through—and the longer it cooks, the juicier it is!—not all the recipes can be cooked in less than thirty minutes. But those that require a little longer are oven dishes, so you can pop them in, and go about your business. No stovetop hovering and stirring and worrying required!

And none of the recipes use more than ten ingredients (not counting staples like salt, pepper, and oil). More than half of my recipes actually use less than seven ingredients, and most of them can be made with what you already have at home!

Quick prep and fast meals means more time to savor your friends, your family, and your food—better for your relationships and great for your body since eating slower aids digestion and encourages you to eat less. Win-win-win!

FIT

All of the recipes in this book are also low-fat and low-cholesterol. And I'm giving you complete nutritional information for every single recipe so you can accurately plan for your healthy lifestyle, weight-loss goal, or work within your weight management program. And don't worry, there's not a rice cake or wheatgrass shot in sight. It's all good Italian food!

I was lucky enough to grow up with parents from Italy who brought their Mediterranean culture and cuisine with them. It's been well documented that the Mediterranean diet is one of the best regional diets on the planet. The Mayo Clinic writes about how "heart-healthy" it is, and how it "reduces incidences of cancer and cancer mortality, Parkinson's and Alzheimer's diseases." *U.S. News and World Report* ranked it one of the "Best Diets Overall" for being easy to follow, safe, and offering diverse foods that help fight against chronic diseases like diabetes. And while other world diets from Japan to the jungle make similar claims, only the Mediterranean diet can prove it.

One of those super smart guys from Harvard, epidemiologist Dimitrios Trichopoulos, told *Forbes* magazine in 2010 that the only diet that's been studied sufficiently to make any such claims is the Mediterranean diet. In 2008, the *British*

✳ ✳ ✳ What Is the Mediterranean Diet? ✳ ✳ ✳

The Mediterranean diet uses fruits, vegetables, grains, and beans as the basis for every single meal. Food is seasoned with herbs and spices rather than salt. Olive oil is used for almost everything instead of butter. Seafood is the primary protein, usually eaten at least three times a week.

It actually has its own cute little food pyramid!

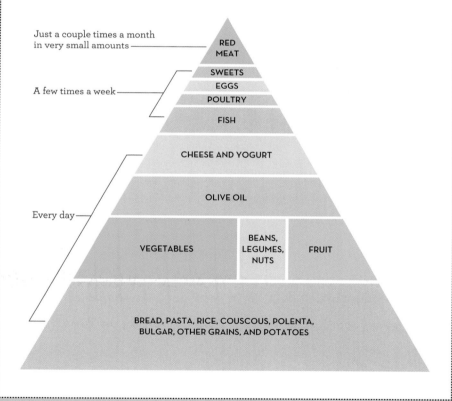

Just a couple times a month in very small amounts ——— RED MEAT

A few times a week ——— SWEETS / EGGS / POULTRY / FISH

CHEESE AND YOGURT

OLIVE OIL

Every day ———

VEGETABLES | BEANS, LEGUMES, NUTS | FRUIT

BREAD, PASTA, RICE, COUSCOUS, POLENTA, BULGAR, OTHER GRAINS, AND POTATOES

Medical Journal analyzed 1.6 million subjects and found that people who eat like *la via Italiana* had a 9 percent lower death rate than people who didn't. Nine percent is a lot! Say you were supposed to kick it at the age of 65—an extra 9 percent would give you 5 more years. Instead of living to be 70, you could live to be 75, maybe walk your great-grandchildren down the aisle.

Trust me, this is the diet you want to be on. But I actually don't like to call it a "diet." To me, a diet is about lots of restrictions and more than a little torture. This is a *lifestyle*—a healthy, active lifestyle that can help you feel better, look amazing, live longer, and hopefully avoid some of the nastier problems that high-fat and high-cholesterol foods leave behind.

FOURTH CHILD

Speaking of behinds, let's talk about mine. I love Audriana dearly, but my fourth pregnancy really did a number on my backside. At first I loved the extra curves, but they just kept curving . . . and curving . . .

It did take me until my fourth baby to really see major changes in my body, but the truth is eventually, it catches up with all of us (at least all of us without secret "C-Tucks"). Sometimes it's after the first baby, sometimes it's the twins that do us in (the baby kind, not the bubbie kind, although I guess those could do it, too . . .). It could be any one or a combination of things: your age, your work, your stress level.

And if it doesn't catch up with you on the outside, you can bet it's gonna catch up with you on the inside. I know plenty of people who are super skinny and eat like crap. You might be able to get away with that when you're fifteen or even twenty-five, but once you hit a certain age, your bad eating habits and lack of exercise will start to show in other places besides your waist: in your skin, your hair, your wrinkles, your inability to recover from an illness quickly, and your overall health.

FORTY

Speaking of "a certain age," everyone has one. And I just hit mine. My last (and certainly not my favorite!) F-word: "Forty."

Everything they say about getting older is true: You have to work harder for smaller results. I'll be honest, I never had to exercise before. That has since changed. I know I'm lucky to only be getting hit with this now, but I promise you, it hit me! And it hit me where it hurts: blown up on Page Six. Tell you the truth, it's not easy being a normal girl in an abnormal world. I'm constantly at events next to big-name celebrities with tiny, tiny waists. I have to remind myself that they had their secret surgeries; they have personal chefs who prepare them "bites" instead of "meals"; they're wearing three pairs of Spanx.

Aside from having another baby and turning forty, I went back to work, and I let my healthy-eating guard down. I now realize I grew up in a bubble of Old World Italy with a mom who stayed home and cooked every meal from scratch for me and my brother. Every meal, every day, was authentic, Italian healthy. We never went to McDonald's. We hardly ever ate out. Eating lots of fruits and vegetables and fresh fish was second nature to me, and I carried those good habits with me as I grew older.

Until recently.

My work schedule became a travel itinerary as I started crisscrossing the country for filming and appearances and (somewhat ironically) to promote my book (which was all about the benefits of home cooking). Room service, restaurants, fast food, airport food . . . it all slowly started creeping into my life. I swear to you I had no idea there was so much fattening, tempting, and terrible food out there! I know that sounds crazy, but I went from living with my mom to living with my husband. I took my own lunches to work in the city, and then I was a stay-at-home mom. Authentic Italian food was my whole life. I never knew any different.

✳ ✳ ✳ Sexy Substitutions ✳ ✳ ✳

I receive so many letters from people asking if my recipes will work with their special diets, and I'm happy to say they will!

Vegetarian

While almost half of my recipes are already vegetarian, you can easily swap out the meat for your favorite veggie or meat substitute in the rest.

Gluten Free

I'm happy to report that every single recipe in this book can be made gluten-free. In fact, since I'm all about fresh veggies and moderate amounts of meat, and we're making everything from scratch so there aren't any sneaky additives, most of the recipes in this book already are gluten-free. In pasta recipes, you can use gluten-free pasta or substitute rice; toast gluten-free bread for bruschetta; and use gluten-free breadcrumbs (Rice Krispies® Gluten Free cereal would give the same yummy crunch as panko) and you're all set!

Weight Watchers®

Since I'm including full nutritional information for every recipe in the back (see page 176), you can easily use your little slide ruler or online calculator to find the points value.

Veal

Any time you see veal, it can easily be replaced with chicken. Or even try using large eggplant slices to go full vegetarian.

I want you to know I get it. (Finally, right?) Crappy food might have crept into your life in college, you might have grown up on fish sticks and french fries like a lot of my girlfriends, or maybe you were blessed for decades, but the older we get and the more garbage they put on the supermarket shelves posing as food, the harder it's getting for all of us.

I now haul my (hopefully shrinking) butt to the gym every morning after I drop the girls off at school. I should have been doing that all these years anyway just for my heart health. And after a brief detour on the dark side, I am back to eating 100% healthy Italian food.

FOREVER FOOD

I introduced this style of my family's cooking to you (and celebrated all the fun that could be had with the food) in my previous book. But with this book, I really want to teach you how to make it a permanent part of your lifestyle. This isn't a short-term diet. It's a lifelong commitment to healthier living.

You can certainly find unhealthy Italian food—especially Italian-American food and especially anything served at a certain restaurant chain that shall not be named (initials: O.G.). But you won't find it in this book! Here, I'm going to teach you how to think, shop, cook, eat, live, and love your body like an Italian.

Because believe me, there is no better way.

CHAPTER 1

Kitchen Catechism

We've established that all the recipes in this book are fast and fit: less than ten ingredients, less than thirty minutes to prepare, low-fat, and low-cholesterol. But hear me clearly, they are still fabulous because they are my family recipes, and they are definitely delicious, because otherwise, what's the point?

I'm never going to be the girl to give you recipes for tofu and soy milk meatballs. *Non mi va;* that's just not me. I've never made something with agave or even Splenda®. I'm sure they're wonderful, I just didn't grow up eating that way, and I don't cook that way now.

I promise you don't have to live on cabbage soup to stay healthy. You don't have to turn vegan or swear off dairy. (But if you do have a special diet, it's still easy to work with my recipes as most of them are already vegetarian, or can be, and are also easily made gluten-free). You can still have pasta, cheese, bread, and even pancetta as long as you follow a few simple rules.

✶✶✶ Wholesome Threesome ✶✶✶

Save money and always have fresh herbs on hand by growing these three Italian staples in small pots or in a cute rectangular planter. With a little attention, they'll thrive indoors, year-round, in even the smallest kitchen. (And they'll make your house or apartment smell great!)

· BASIL   · ROSEMARY   · PARSLEY

But these rules are important. Really, really important. Mess them up and you could end up with a heart-clogging disaster worthy of the O.G. (God forbid!) Because they are so important, I'm not even going to call them rules. (Since I know a good number of you, like myself, like to break the rules sometimes!) But these rules should not be broken! So I'm giving them a fancy church name inspired by my girls just starting CCD classes again. They are *canons*: things you must commit to memory, recite to yourself as you brave the grocery store aisles, and follow every single day if you want to have a healthy, heavenly bod. (Don't worry, they're easy and fun!)

Canon 1:
IT ALL STARTS AT THE STORE

No matter how many culinary tricks you try, you can't turn food that's unhealthy to start with into healthy food. Baking a Twinkie cake versus deep-frying it might make it healthier, but it will never make it healthy. (And there's a big, big difference!) If you don't start with good stuff, you certainly won't end up with it.

Since most of us don't live on a farm, preparing meals first means a trip to the place where food is sold. If you're lucky, you have a farmers' market near you. Go there and buy everything you possibly can! When you have to go to the grocery store (with four girls it seems like I'm there every other day!), be a conscientious shopper. Don't let the brightly packaged junk or super sales on crazy crap distract you. You are there on a holy mission: to get the best food possible to nourish your body, mind, and soul.

To stay focused and find the right food, work your way through the store in a giant figure-8. Make a big loop on the perimeter of the store through the produce section and meat counters. Cut through the center aisle for dried herbs and pastas only. Then finish the second loop by swinging past the dairy and egg section. Avoid all the other aisles of processed food and sugary snacks. Don't even walk down them so you won't be tempted (if I have to cut through an aisle, I always shoot down the dog food aisle!).

And never shop on an empty stomach; you'll end up buying junk you don't need because your judgment will be compromised by your grumbling tummy. Grab a healthy snack at home before you go.

Canon 2:
HEALTHY FOOD DOESN'T HAVE A LABEL

So you're in the store and you're determined to only buy healthy things. Good for you! But what makes something healthy? The packaging and labels are so confusing, and as soon as we figure out the evil ingredients, the food manufacturers go and change the names of them to trick us.

Corn-fusing

The more processed food is, the less healthy it becomes. When word got out that high fructose corn syrup wasn't good for you, people stopped buying products containing it. And of course the folks that make it, don't like that. So they just changed the name. Now they call it "corn sugar." The FDA hasn't yet decided if manufacturers are allowed to label products with high fructose corn syrup as just

---

* * * The Opposite is True * * *

While you can't take unhealthy food and make it healthy, it's certainly possible to take healthy food and muck it up. (Just ask the O.G.) If you make sure there's only good stuff in your cart, I promise I'll walk you through how to turn it into delicious and healthy meals!

containing "corn sugar" (which is misleading because it sounds like two natural, non-processed ingredients), but that hasn't stopped the industry from running television ads touting the sparkly new name. While the experts debate this for the next several years, what are we supposed to do?

Simple. You'll never be caught by a misleading label if you remember Canon #2: The healthiest food you can buy doesn't even have a label.

Think about it: fruits, vegetables, fresh fish from the market. No labels. You don't have to worry about what's been squirted inside or dyed or added. (If you buy packaged meat, look for organic, grass-fed, no-hormones-added choices.)

If the majority of your diet consists of food that doesn't have a label, you're on a good, healthy path.

Canon 3:
EXTRA-VIRGIN IS THE ONLY WAY TO GO

I've written a lot about (blessed) virgin olive oil in my other books, and I'm going to write some more. If your body is a temple, then it only makes sense that it should be full of virgin. Extra-virgin olive oil is the ONLY oil you should use. For cooking, marinating, drizzling over salads, and even baking, there is nothing better.

Olive oil is essentially a natural, nonprocessed juice pressed from olives. Extra-virgin means it's pure and the highest quality. Nothing else matters on the label, just those words: extra-virgin olive oil.

Extra-virgin olive oil is more than just a good alternative to other fats. Its monounsaturated fatty acids are believed to lower your risk of heart disease, stroke, help control blood sugar levels, reduce blood pressure, benefit your digestive system, even help with arthritis. It's good for your skin, your hair, and it tastes delicious!

All of my recipes, even the desserts, use only extra-virgin olive oil.

Canon 4:
SIZE MATTERS

Bigger is better in many areas, but not when it comes to what you eat. Portion size is everything. You can enjoy your favorite foods—delicious pastas with divine sauces, sizzling steaks, even creamy desserts—as long as you eat normal-sized servings.

In America, everything has gotten supersized, even our dinner plates. It's hard to remember what a "normal" serving size should look like. Here's a quick cheat: look at your hands. Cup your palm: that's one serving size. Unless you have freaky baby hands, your body is naturally designed to tell you how much you need to eat. Adult men have bigger hands and should get bigger portions; kids should have kid-hand-sized portions. A well-balanced meal has one hand of protein and two hands of vegetables.

Canon 5:
THE MORE COLORFUL YOUR FOOD, THE BETTER

Kids breakfast cereal aside, good healthy food is colorful. A plate full of white or beige or even brown food probably has a lot of white flour, starch, and unhealthy fat. You want lots of bright primary colors: greens, reds, yellows, purples. What does that mean? Lots of fruits and vegetables!

I like to dress up my dinner the way I dress up myself: pretty with lots of colors. I don't want to live my life dressed in drab, depressing clothes. And I don't want to eat that way either. A hot red dress makes you feel sexy and confident. A hot red pepper should, too.

ITALIAN PANTRY STAPLES, AKA INGREDIENTS(ES)

One of the great things about authentic Italian cooking is its simplicity. You use a minimum amount of ingredients for maximum taste, the ingredients are inexpensive, and you get to use them over and over again.

Make sure your cupboard is stocked with the following (no cumin required!), and with your favorite fresh or frozen meats and veggies, you can create hundreds of spectacular dishes:

Liquids:

- Extra-virgin olive oil (only extra-virgin, preferably bottled in Italy)
- Vinegar: Balsamic and Red Wine
- Broth: Chicken/Vegetable and Beef (always reduced-sodium)
- Wine: Dry White, Red, and Marsala*

Dried Herbs:

- Fennel seeds, whole
- Hot red pepper flakes, crushed
- Peppercorns, whole

- Garlic powder
- Oregano
- Thyme

Fresh Herbs:

- Basil
- Rosemary or Sage

- Parsley
- Thyme

✳ ✳ ✳ Crushing Spices and Herbs ✳ ✳ ✳

Some spices (such as fennel seeds) I buy whole only because they are used in recipes that way. And if I need them crushed, I just crush them myself: Put them in a plastic bag, cover with a dishtowel, and whack with a rolling pin. Dried herbs are delicate and easy to crush with your fingertips.

✳ ✳ ✳ Storing Fresh Herbs ✳ ✳ ✳

Basil is delicate, and can turn black if exposed to cold refrigerator air. It's best to store it outside of the fridge, with the stems trimmed, in a glass of water, just like a bouquet. Other fresh herbs can be stored in the refrigerator crisper. Rinse, dry, and chop them just before you use them. If you plan to sprinkle the herbs as a garnish, pat them dry with paper towels or spin in the salad spinner before chopping; wet chopped herbs will clump and not sprinkle nicely, but when rinsed and thoroughly dried, they make you look like a pro.

Aromatics:

• Garlic • Onions • Shallots

Cans/Boxes:

• Cans of Diced Tomatoes

• Cans of Tomato Paste

• Cans of Whole Tomatoes

• Cans of Plain Tomato Sauce

• Breadcrumbs: Panko, Plain, and Italian Seasoned**

Frozen:

• Artichoke hearts • Corn

• Lima beans (good substitute • Peas

  for fava beans)

*Do not buy "cooking" wines as they are full of salt and preservatives and will ruin your dish. You can get a nice bottle you wouldn't mind drinking for less than $7 and it will last you through many, many recipes.

**An opened can of breadcrumbs can be stored in the refrigerator or freezer for over a year!

TOMATOES: DIVINE SELECTION

Unless they're in season at your local farmers' market, fresh tomatoes aren't always the best choice. In fact, the off-season ones in chain grocery stores, even though they're fresh, sometimes aren't in great shape. Thank the heavens for canned tomatoes!

Of course, not all canned tomatoes are created equal. Here's a cheat sheet on what to look for (and what to look out for):

Diced Tomatoes

Diced tomatoes often have preservatives in them to keep the little squares looking pretty. Use them if you need to in things like salsa, but if the tomatoes are just melting into a sauce, skip them and go for whole tomatoes.

Crushed Tomatoes

Crushed tomatoes are often not just whole tomatoes that have been crushed, but the pulpy insides of bits of less-than-perfect tomatoes. Avoid them.

---

* * * Tomato Paste Waste * * *

Even though tomato paste cans are small and inexpensive, I hate throwing away any extra when I only need a spoonful. There are two ways around this. Buy a tube of tomato paste (sold at specialty stores, online, and many supermarkets); it's more expensive, but there's no waste. Or you can scoop the remaining tomato paste from the can into 1-tablespoon globs onto a piece of waxed paper. Put them in the freezer, and when they harden, pop them in a freezer bag. Whenever you need a tablespoon, just grab one from the freezer; they defrost almost instantly.

Whole Tomatoes

For most of my cooking, I use cans of whole tomatoes, and I use the juices in the can, too. And to cut them up, you can stick a pair of kitchen scissors right into the can and snip away, or be like a professional chef and squish the tomatoes into pieces with your (clean) hands as they slide out of the can. I love San Marzano plum tomatoes, grown in the volcanic soil of Mt. Vesuvius near Naples. They are more expensive than American tomatoes, but I can really taste the difference (the Italian ones are meatier somehow) and I bet you will, too.

Tomato Paste vs. Purée

Tomato paste is a thick, concentrated paste of tomatoes. You add a small amount to thicken and flavor sauces and soups. Tomato purée is more like a soup itself because it's watered down. We only want the paste.

Tomato Sauce

If you don't have jars of your own homemade tomato sauce sitting around (or if you usually do, but you ran out, which is what happens to me every year) and you need a good amount of sauce for a dish like lasagna, canned tomato sauce is great. It gives you bulk, but allows you to add the flavor.

Nothing Extra

You want canned tomatoes in any form to list just a couple things on the ingredients list, hopefully just tomatoes and sometimes tomato juice. Salt is okay unless you're on a sodium-restricted diet, and then you should opt for "no salt" varieties and season it yourself. A lot of companies also include citric acid or calcium chloride—some say it's "naturally occurring"—which are preservatives to keep the food from spoiling. It's supposedly not bad for you, but you can find options without it. Definitely avoid any cans with high fructose corn syrup or chemicals you can't pronounce!

No Flavorings

You want plain tomatoes. You'll add the flavoring yourself. Don't get tomatoes with basil or garlic or any other extras.

GIVE IT UP:
THE 3 FOODS YOU MUST AVOID

Before we get to the good stuff, I have to give you one more little list: the foods you seriously need to cut out of your diet right now. They're no good for you. They never will be.

1. Vegetable Oil

I know I preach about extra-virgin olive oil (which is technically a "fruit oil"), but I'm so serious about it, I want to make sure you know to never use its ugly alternative: vegetable oil. Like "corn sugar," vegetable oil is a misleading label. Yes, vegetables are very healthy. No, the stuff in vegetable oil is nothing like a vegetable. All the nutrients are sucked out, crazy trans fats (also labeled "partially hydrogenated fats") are stuffed in, and the vegetables they use in the first place are often genetically modified.

Do not sauté in it. Do not deep-fry with it. Do not pour cups of it into your baked goods. If you can't use extra-virgin olive oil, go for canola, which is made from a seed, not a vegetable (although it's a genetically modified seed, so I skip it).

2. Shortening

I'll be honest, I think shortening is the devil. I know it's great for making homemade

∗ ∗ ∗ Storage Success ∗ ∗ ∗

Once you've filled your kitchen with the right food, we want to make sure it lasts as long as possible. Here's a quick chart on how to store what, where, and for how long.

FRESH WHOLE TOMATOES
- Store in a single layer on the counter, stems down.
- Do not refrigerate, as cold will cause the tomato to get mealy and lose its flavor.
- Up to 1 week

FRESH CUT TOMATOES
- Store cut-side down on a small plate on the counter.
- 1–2 days

ONIONS*
- Cool, dark place (not the fridge) in a breathable container (not plastic bag!).
- 1–2 weeks

CUT ONIONS
- In a sealed container in the refrigerator.
- 7–10 days

POTATOES*
- Cool, dark place (not the fridge) in a breathable container (not plastic bag!).
- 1–2 weeks

CUT POTATOES
- Will only last up to 2 hours, so use 'em up once you cut 'em!

GARLIC
- Cool, dark place in a breathable container (garlic pots are great!).
- Up to 3 months

DRIED PASTA
- Cool, dark place. Should be put in an airtight container once box is opened.
- Up to 1 year

CANNED TOMATOES/TOMATO PASTE
- In the cupboard.
- Up to 1 year

*Do not store onions and potatoes in the same basket, as the onions will suck the moisture out of the potatoes.

Entertainment

One of the ways I keep myself motivated for working out, especially on the treadmill, is to only allow myself to catch up on my favorite television shows if I'm exercising at the same time. There are big TVs at my gym, the iPad is great for watching shows—I can even get them on my phone. No pain, no *Dancing with the Stars* gain!

biscuits and fried chicken, but those aren't healthy foods by a long shot, so you should probably give those up anyway.

Shortening is nothing but vegetable oil in a scarier solid form with no taste and plenty of stuff your body doesn't know what to do with. Exorcise this demon from your cupboard. Butter will work as a substitute in any recipe that calls for shortening that you just can't live without.

3. Fake Butter

Margarine and butter substitutes may have less saturated fat than real butter, but a lot of times they have more trans fats, and all the time they have tons of chemicals. Like I-Can't-Believe-It's-Not-Plastic amounts of chemicals. If something claiming to be "food" never, ever spoils and even bugs won't eat it, you probably shouldn't either.

I use extra-virgin olive oil every chance I get, but if I have to use butter, I only use real butter (and I use it in moderation). Real butter is nothing but cream, milk, and maybe some water. Buy only Grade AA. For baking, I use unsalted butter so I can control the amount of salt in the recipe. For spreading, I use Land O'Lakes Butter with Olive Oil. It's spreadable like butter and only has three ingredients: cream, olive oil, and salt. And thanks to the olive oil, it also has 50 percent less cholesterol and 45 percent less saturated fat that regular butter.

CHAPTER 2

Live It Up—
I-Can't-Believe-It's-Not-Fattening Food

I just gave you the lowdown on the foods you should give up, so it's only fair to start off with scrumptious healthy dishes that allow you to live it up!

I have gotten so many cookbooks to try something new—like Indian cuisine or Middle Eastern—and they jump right into crazy, complicated instructions and ingredients I've never heard of and I'll be honest, it puts me off.

I know not everyone grew up eating the same Italian vegetables I did—like escarole and chard. Maybe the only beans you ate were the kind that came in a can with franks. It doesn't matter; we'll start nice and slow. These recipes all have ingredients you'll recognize that are guaranteed picky-eater approved, with easy instructions and an outcome that will have you amazed.

These dishes are so good, you won't believe they're healthy. But I promise they are. (Check out the Nutritional Information on page 176.) With careful selection of the right ingredients, some cooking savvy, and portion control, you can eat like a king and still have a hot, healthy body.

✻✻✻ When in Rome . . . The Sequel ✻✻✻

In my previous cookbooks, I taught you the correct pronunciation of Italian food (and my last name), and my daughter Milania taught you how to count in Italian. So now I want to teach you more conversational Italian. *Capisce?* (You understand?). *Ecco* (EK-oh) is our way of saying "voilà."

Chicken with Bruschetta Topping

Makes 4 servings

I had to put this one first because it's my favorite recipe in this book. Like my children, I love them all, but this one just has a special place in my heart (and like one of my children, it happened by accident—kidding!). I'm always mixing and matching ingredients in the kitchen; one day, I mixed up a bruschetta topping but ran out of bread, so I pulled some chicken breasts from the freezer and *ecco!*

3 ripe plum (Roma) tomatoes,
seeded and cut into ½-inch dice
½ cup finely chopped onion
1 medium celery rib,
cut into ¼-inch dice
¼ cup dry white wine
2 tablespoons chopped fresh
Italian parsley
2 tablespoons extra-virgin olive oil,
plus more for the pan
2 garlic cloves, minced
¼ teaspoon red pepper flakes
4 boneless, skinless chicken breast
halves (about 1½ pounds)
¼ teaspoon salt
¼ teaspoon freshly ground
black pepper

1. Position a rack in the upper third of the oven and preheat the oven to 450ºF. Lightly oil a 13 x 9-inch baking pan.

2. Combine the tomatoes, onion, celery, wine, parsley, oil, garlic, and red pepper flakes in a medium bowl. Set aside while the oven is preheating.

3. One at a time, place a chicken breast half between 2 plastic storage bags. Using a flat meat pounder or a rolling pin, pound the chicken until it is ½-inch thick. Season with the salt and black pepper.

4. Arrange the chicken in the prepared baking pan. Spoon equal amounts of the tomato mixture over each chicken breast half, then pour any of the liquid in the bowl around the chicken. Bake until the tomato mixture is hot and the chicken is opaque throughout, 15 to 20 minutes.

5. Transfer each chicken breast half with its topping to a dinner plate, then pour the pan juices on top. Serve hot.

When in Rome . . .	*When in Jersey . . .*
Capisce = cah-PEE-shuh	Capisce = cah-PEESH

✳ ✳ ✳ **Waist Not** ✳ ✳ ✳

One of the reasons I love bruschetta so much is because of what it represents: Italian frugality. Especially in the Old Country, and certainly in my house, we pride ourselves on not wasting anything. We like nice things of course, but the cheaper you can get them, the better. No joke, I get a lot of my designer clothes at T. J. Maxx (they have such a great one at the Shore!). I would never, ever pay full price—or even close!—for a pair of fancy shoes. Are you kidding me? You *walk* on them! Who cares about a red sole once you get it all scuffed up?

And we never waste food! *Madonna Mia*, the thought! Bruschetta was invented to use up stale bread. My husband, Joe, just made homemade applesauce yesterday with some apples that were going bad. We had some last night as a dessert, and again today for breakfast!

Everyone knows Italians make huge amounts of food, but here's our secret: We don't eat huge amounts. We make a lot because it saves money and time, and because we want the leftovers! Italian food gets better the next day. The longer it sits in the herbs and olive oil, the juicier it gets. My family, we might eat the same thing in slightly different forms for three days in a row.

All of the recipes I'm giving you are quick to make, but if you want to double (or even triple) the recipes for leftovers, I promise you they're magic!

✳ ✳ ✳

Joe's Homemade Applesauce

"It's real easy. You just peel, core, and slice up some apples. Stick 'em in a pot and pour enough water over them to just barely cover 'em. Put it over low heat, and simmer them until they're mushy. Don't add anything, no sugar, no nothing. That's it! You can refrigerate it for up a to a week. And it works just as well with pears; maybe even mix the apples with pears."— Joe

Pasta al Forno

Makes 6 servings

Al forno means "from the oven" in Italian, so it can describe almost any baked dish. This is one of my favorites because it's quick, rich, and makes great leftovers. This is my veggie version, but feel free to make this your own by adding lean meats, such as some cooked Italian turkey sausage or chicken chunks.

1 tablespoon extra-virgin olive oil

1 medium onion, finely chopped

1 red bell pepper, seeded, cored, and cut into ¼-inch dice

10 ounces cremini mushrooms, thinly sliced

2 garlic cloves, minced

1 (28-ounce) can crushed tomatoes

2 teaspoons Italian seasoning

1 pound whole-wheat penne rigate pasta

1 cup pitted and coarsely chopped kalamata olives

1 cup low-fat ricotta cheese

¼ cup freshly grated Parmigiano-Reggiano or Parmesan cheese

1. Preheat the oven to 350ºF. Lightly oil a 13 x 9-inch baking dish.

2. Bring a large pot of lightly salted water to a boil over high heat.

3. Meanwhile, heat the oil in a large saucepan over medium heat. Add the onion and red bell pepper and cook, stirring occasionally, until softened, about 3 minutes. Add the mushrooms and increase the heat to medium-high. Cook, stirring occasionally, until the mushrooms are sizzling in their own juices, about 6 minutes. Stir in the garlic and cook until fragrant, about 1 minute. Add the crushed tomatoes and Italian seasoning and bring to a simmer. Reduce the heat to medium and cook, stirring occasionally, until slightly thickened, about 15 minutes.

4. Add the pasta to the water and cook according to the package directions until al dente. Drain well. Return the pasta to its cooking pot. Add the tomato mixture, olives, and ricotta and stir well. Spread in the prepared baking dish and sprinkle with the Parmesan cheese.

5. Bake until the Parmesan is melted, about 20 minutes. Let stand for 5 minutes. Serve hot.

Chicken Milanese

Makes 4 servings

I love anything named after my favorite city on earth (and the inspiration for Milania's name!), but here's a healthier take on the usual pan-fried chicken. I use half panko breadcrumbs for extra crunch, and half Italian-seasoned breadcrumbs for flavor. Serve it like they do in Milan, on a bed of undressed baby greens or arugula with lemon wedges.

4 boneless, skinless chicken
    breast halves, pounded to
    ½-inch thickness
½ cup all-purpose flour
2 large egg whites
1 cup Italian-seasoned breadcrumbs
1 cup panko breadcrumbs
2 tablespoons Pecorino Romano,
    Parmigiano-Reggiano, or
    Parmesan cheese, freshly grated
¼ cup finely chopped fresh
    Italian parsley
3 tablespoons extra-virgin olive oil
½ lemon

1. Pat chicken breasts dry with paper towel. Put flour in shallow dish. Set aside. Whisk egg whites in new shallow dish. Set aside. Mix Italian breadcrumbs, panko, cheese, and parsley in third shallow dish. Set aside.

2. Coat each chicken breast one at a time. First, dredge the chicken in flour, shaking off any excess, then dip chicken in egg. Then press chicken into breadcrumb mixture, turning to coat evenly. Set the coated chicken on a baking sheet and let stand for 5 minutes to set the coating so it stays on during cooking.

3. Heat the oil in a large sauté pan over medium-high heat. Sauté the chicken for 3 to 5 minutes on each side, until lightly browned and an instant-read thermometer inserted through the side of a breast half into the center reads 165ºF.

4. Serve immediately with fresh lemon squeezed over the top.

Fettuccine alla Carbonara

Makes 6 servings

The secret to this fabulous dish is its simplicity. While it seems to have a cream sauce, there's no cream involved. Eggs cooked by the hot pasta create these shimmering noodles, seasoned with crispy pancetta. For extra veggies, add a cup of fresh or frozen peas. Heaven on a plate!

3 ounces thick-sliced pancetta, cut into ¼-inch dice

1 tablespoon extra-virgin olive oil

1 medium onion, finely chopped

2 garlic cloves, minced

1 pound fettuccine pasta

2 large eggs

2 large egg whites

¾ cup freshly grated Parmigiano-Reggiano or Parmesan cheese

¼ teaspoon freshly ground black pepper

1. Bring a large pot of lightly salted water to a boil over high heat.

2. Meanwhile, cook the pancetta and oil together in a medium skillet over medium heat, stirring occasionally, until the pancetta begins to brown, about 3 minutes. Add the onion and cook, stirring occasionally, until the onion is tender, about 3 minutes more. Stir in the garlic and cook until it is fragrant, about 1 minute. Transfer to a bowl and let cool until tepid.

3. Add the fettuccine to the water and cook, stirring occasionally, according to the package directions until al dente. Scoop out and reserve about 1 cup of the pasta cooking liquid. Drain the pasta well. Return the pasta to its cooking pot.

4. Add the eggs, egg whites, Parmesan cheese, and pepper to the onion mixture and mix well with a fork. Stirring the pasta in the pot, mix in the egg mixture, then enough of the pasta cooking water to make a creamy sauce. Transfer to pasta bowls and serve hot.

✱✱✱ A Little Pancetta Goes a Long Way ✱✱✱

While pancetta and its American cousin bacon are both made from pork belly, they don't taste the same because they are prepared differently. Bacon is smoked; pancetta is cured. While neither one is healthy in large quantities, we don't use them that way in healthy Italian cooking. We use it in small amounts for big flavor. My Fettuccine alla Carbonara calls for just ½ ounce of pancetta per serving.

If you'd like, you can substitute turkey bacon, but I don't for two reasons: Turkey bacon has a lot of sodium and comes in big packages. You can buy tiny amounts of pancetta at the deli counter, use only what you need, and not have to worry about the rest of the package calling your name from the fridge.

Tight, Toned Arms

My favorite season is summer, and I love wearing sleeveless shirts and dresses. A quick way to tone your arms without using weights (do it in the kitchen while you're waiting for dinner to finish cooking!) is a simple exercise I call *abbracci*. Abbracci means "hugs" in Italian, and the little circles you make in the air remind me of the o's when you write "xoxo" for kisses and hugs. (And it reminds me that if I keep on my arm toning, I won't be embarrassed by flabby arms when I give someone a hug!) It's super-easy. Here's how to do it:

- Stand with your feet shoulder-width apart. Suck in your stomach and hold it tight.

- Hold your arms straight out at your shoulders, palms facing the ceiling, fingers together.

- Move your arms forward in small, fast circles. (Think about drawing tiny circles in the air with the bottom of your wrists.) Continue until you can't do any more.

- Change direction and do it again until you can't do any more.

- Rest your arms for a couple of minutes, then do two more sets. (You can also do this sitting in a chair if you need to, just make sure you have plenty of room around you.)

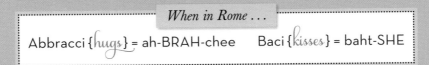

When in Rome . . .

Abbracci {*hugs*} = ah-BRAH-chee   Baci {*kisses*} = baht-SHE

Veal Stew Osso Buco–Style

Makes 6 servings

Another specialty from Milan, osso buco is a veal shank braised in broth and wine. In a lot of places, it's served as a huge hunk of meat, but to be healthier (and save money!), I make it the traditional way they did on farms in Italy: as a stew with lots of veggies and meat for flavoring. Baking a stew in the oven means you don't have to babysit it on top of the stove, and worry that it is going to scorch on the bottom.

2 tablespoons extra-virgin olive oil, divided

2 1/2 pounds boneless veal shoulder, cut into 1-inch chunks

2 teaspoons salt

1 teaspoon freshly ground black pepper

1 medium onion, chopped

2 medium carrots, cut into 1/2-inch dice

2 medium celery ribs, cut into 1/2-inch dice

3 garlic cloves, minced, divided

1 cup dry white wine

1 (28-ounce) can Italian plum tomatoes with their juices, chopped

2 teaspoons Italian seasoning

4 tablespoons finely chopped fresh Italian parsley, divided

Grated zest of 1 lemon

1. Preheat the oven to 350ºF.

2. Heat 1 tablespoon of oil in a large Dutch oven or flameproof casserole over medium-high heat. Season the veal with the salt and pepper. In batches, add the veal and cook, stirring occasionally, until lightly browned, about 5 minutes. Transfer to a plate.

3. Add the remaining 1 tablespoon oil to the Dutch oven over medium heat. Add the onion, carrots, celery, and 2 chopped garlic cloves and cover. Cook, stirring occasionally to loosen the browned bits in the pan, until the vegetables are softened, about 10 minutes. Add the wine, scraping up more of the browned bits, and bring to a boil. Stir in the tomatoes and their juices, Italian seasoning, and 2 tablespoons of parsley. Return the veal to the Dutch oven and bring to a boil. Cover tightly.

4. Bake until the veal is tender, about 1 1/2 hours. Mix the remaining 2 tablespoons parsley and minced garlic with the lemon zest in a small bowl. Sprinkle over the veal stew and serve hot.

> ∗ ∗ ∗ **Gremolata** ∗ ∗ ∗
>
> The fresh parsley, garlic, and lemon zest mixture is called *gremolata*. It adds a blast of fresh flavor to the stew, so don't skip it. It's also great over seafood. Use gremolata, and you'll be a true Italian cook!

Roasted Pork Loin with Peppercorn Crust

Makes 8 servings

This is Joe's specialty and yes, it's juicy and delicious! The peppercorn crust gives it a crunchy, zesty texture on the outside, while the inside is melt-in-your-mouth smooth. You could also throw this on the grill.

1 boneless center-cut pork loin
   (3 pounds)
2 tablespoons extra-virgin
   olive oil, divided
1½ teaspoons salt, divided
1 tablespoon black peppercorns,
   coarsely cracked in a mortar
½ cup finely chopped onion
2 garlic cloves, finely chopped
12 medium-sized red, purple,
   and gold potatoes (2 pounds),
   cut lengthwise into quarters
½ cup dry white wine

1. Preheat the oven to 350ºF. Lightly oil a metal roasting pan. Put a roasting rack in the pan.

2. Brush the pork with 1 tablespoon of the olive oil and season with 1 teaspoon of the salt. Place the pork on the roasting rack. Mix the peppercorns, onion, and garlic in a small bowl. Press the peppercorn mixture evenly over the top of the pork. Toss the potatoes with the remaining tablespoon oil in a large bowl, and scatter the potatoes around the pork.

3. Bake, turning the potatoes after 45 minutes, until an instant-read thermometer inserted in the center of the pork reads 150ºF, about 1 hour and 15 minutes. Transfer the pork to a platter. Sprinkle the potatoes in the pan with the remaining ½ teaspoon salt and transfer to the platter. Tent with aluminum foil to keep warm.

4. To make a sauce with the pan juices, transfer the roasting pan to the stovetop and heat over high heat until the juices sizzle. Add the wine and bring to a boil, scraping up the browned bits in the pan. Cook until the wine is reduced by half, about 3 minutes. Remove from the heat.

5. Cut the pork crosswise into ½-inch slices. Drizzle the sauce over the pork and serve.

✴ ✴ ✴ Crack-a-Lackin' ✴ ✴ ✴

If you don't have a mortar and pestle, you can always crush whole peppercorns using a baking sheet and a heavy pan. Just put the peppercorns on the tray (the rims will keep the peppercorns from rolling away), set a heavy pan or skillet on top, push down with your gorgeous arms, and crush!

CHAPTER 3

Serve It Up—
Amazing Antipasti

In Italy, the antipasto course is just as important as the main course because it helps set the tone for the meal and the evening. Rather than just show up, sit down, and start stuffing your face, the tradition of appetizers as a first, casual course gives everyone time to mingle, slow down from their busy day, and amp up their appetites.

Antipasto dishes are meant to be just small bites to get your metabolism started, not huge plates of food. Yes, there are some traditional fried Italian antipasti, but there are just as many healthy alternatives. Fresh fruits and vegetables with healthy dips are almost always served, along with small seafood like shrimp and clams. Rather than sitting down, Italians walk around sampling antipasti, having loud, loving conversations, and usually drinking wine.

Whether you're hosting a crowd or dining *per due*, beginning with an antipasto (or two) is the perfect way to start your night.

When in Rome . . .

Here are some traditional Italian greetings:
Benvenuti a casa mia! {*Welcome to my home!*} = been-VAY-new-tee AH cah-sa me-YAH
Buonasera {*Good evening*} = boon-AH-ser-ah
Sei così bella. {*You look so pretty.*} = say co-SEE BAY-la
Mangia! Mangia! {*Eat! Eat!*} = man-JAH, man-JAH

Clams Casino

Makes 24 clams, 6 servings

My dad makes better clams casino than anyone on the planet. Well, anyone I've ever met anyway. The secret is to save the clam juice for the stuffing, and to use more clam meat than you use shells so each one is extra stuffed. Unless you have someone in your life who is a master clam shucker and can do them at home, buy the clams on the half shell from your fish guy.

36 littleneck or cherrystone clams,
    shucked, on the half shell,
    juices reserved
3/4 cup dried plain breadcrumbs
2 tablespoons finely chopped fresh
    Italian parsley
2 tablespoons extra-virgin olive oil
3 slices pancetta
    (about 2 3/4 ounces), unrolled
    and cut into 24 pieces

1. Position a rack in the top third of the oven and pre-heat the oven to 450ºF. Tear off 2 sheets of aluminum foil to fit your broiler pan. Loosely crush the foil to fit in the pan. The crumpled foil will hold the clam shells upright during baking.

2. Remove the meat from 12 clams and discard the shells. Coarsely chop the clam meat and transfer to a medium bowl.

3. Add the breadcrumbs, parsley, 2 tablespoons of the reserved clam juices, and the oil to the bowl and mix to make a moist, but not wet, and crumbly paste. Spoon equal amounts of the breadcrumb mixture over the remaining 24 clams in their shells. Nestle the clams, stuffed-side up, in the foil. Top each with a piece of pancetta.

4. Bake until the pancetta and stuffing are browned, about 15 minutes. Serve hot.

✳ ✳ ✳ **Dirty Clams** ✳ ✳ ✳

While no one is sure exactly who invented clams casino, it's the name that makes me giggle. In Italian, *casino* either refers to a big "mess" or a "brothel." I don't think clams casino are all that messy, so I have to wonder....

Ciambotta

Makes 8 servings

Ciambotta refers to different dishes in different parts of Italy; depending on where you are, it can be anything from a spread to a soup. In Salerno, where my parents are from, ciambotta is an eggplant mixture you serve with crusty bread, crackers, or with celery sticks as a dip. Try to make it in the morning and serve it a few hours later so the flavors get a chance to know each other. This is the recipe I used in a cook-off against some of my "Housewife" castmates. It wins every time!

¼ cup extra-virgin olive oil

4 large garlic cloves, quartered

1 medium eggplant
(about 1¼ pounds), cut into
1-inch chunks

4 ripe plum (Roma) tomatoes,
seeded and diced

1 teaspoon garlic powder

¾ teaspoon salt

¼ teaspoon red pepper flakes
(optional)

1. Heat the oil with the garlic in a large skillet over medium-high heat until the garlic is just golden, about 2 minutes. Add the eggplant (it will soak up the oil) and reduce the heat to medium. Cook, stirring often, until the eggplant is tender and releases some of the oil it soaked up, about 10 minutes.

2. Move the eggplant to one side of the skillet. Place the tomatoes on the empty side of the skillet. Sprinkle the tomatoes with the garlic powder and salt. Cook, stirring the tomatoes often, until they give off some of their juices, about 2 minutes. Add the red pepper flakes, if using. Mix the eggplant and tomatoes together and cook, stirring often to scrape up any browned eggplant juices in the skillet, until the tomatoes are tender, about 5 minutes. Serve hot. Or, let the mixture cool, transfer to a bowl, cover, and refrigerate until chilled, about 2 hours.

When in Rome . . .

Ciambotta = cham-BOAT-tah

Creamy Tomato and Basil Dip

Makes about 8 servings (1 cup)

Most dips use either sour cream or mayonnaise, and even though you can get reduced-fat versions, I'd rather not. For super thick and creamy, low-fat dips, I use fat-free cottage cheese. Just purée it in the food processor, add some spice, and dip away! Choose healthy things to dip, though. Raw veggies, whole grain crackers, and bruschette are good. Potato chips, not so much. If you want the dip to be thinner, stir in a little low-fat milk.

2 garlic cloves, crushed with the side of a chef's knife and peeled

1 pint fat-free cottage cheese

1/4 cup drained sun-dried tomatoes in oil, patted dry and coarsely chopped

1/4 cup coarsely chopped fresh basil leaves, plus more for garnish

1/8 teaspoon red pepper flakes

1. With your food processor or blender running, drop the garlic through the feed tube to mince the garlic. Add the cottage cheese and process until smooth.

2. Add the sun-dried tomatoes, 1/4 cup chopped basil, and red pepper flakes and pulse a few times to combine. Cover and refrigerate to blend the flavors for at least 1 hour and up to 1 day. Transfer to a serving bowl, sprinkle with basil, and serve (with healthy dippers!) chilled.

✴ ✴ ✴ 1 Tomato, 2 Tomato ... ✴ ✴ ✴

Bruschetta, the yummy crusty bread with tomato-and-basil topping, actually refers to just one piece. More than one is *bruschette*. Thankfully, they're both pronounced the same: brew-SKET-tah.

Caprese Cherry Tomatoes

Makes 6 servings, 18 tomatoes

Traditionally, caprese salad (named for the island of Capri) is composed of thick slices of tomatoes, thick slices of fresh mozzarella, and fresh basil. I adore that flavor combination, but wanted something with a little less cheese. These baby tomatoes stuffed with just a bite were the perfect solution!

1 pint cherry tomatoes
   (18 tomatoes)
4 ounces reduced-fat cream
   cheese or Neufchâtel cheese,
   softened to room temperature
1 garlic clove, minced
¼ cup shredded part-skim
   mozzarella cheese
1 tablespoon finely chopped
   fresh basil

1. Use a sharp paring knife to cut the top ¼ inch from each cherry tomato, and use the tip of the knife to scoop out the pulp to make a shell. (Save the pulp for sauce or soup, if you wish.) Place the tomatoes cut-side down on paper towels to drain briefly while making the filling.

2. Mash the cream cheese and garlic together in a small bowl with a rubber spatula. Transfer to a 1-quart resealable plastic bag. Snip off a corner of the bag. Use the bag like a pastry bag to pipe the cheese mixture into the cherry tomatoes.

3. Spread the mozzarella cheese in a saucer. Turn each cherry tomato upside-down and dip the cheese filling into the mozzarella so it sticks. Turn right-side up. Sprinkle the tops of the tomatoes with the basil. Cover and refrigerate for up to 4 hours.

When in Rome . . .

Caprese = cah-PREE-zay

Fruit and Prosciutto Crostini

Makes 6 servings, 18 crostini

I know prosciutto and melon is one of the most famous Italian appetizer combinations, but that sweet-salty combination is delicious with all kinds of fruits. In my parents' village, they use juicy pears, peaches, and plums. Here's how to make it with melon or other fruits; just be sure to choose good ripe fruit in season (there's nothing worse than hard, unripe melon, period). If you want, drizzle each with a few drops of aged balsamic vinegar (the good stuff you get at an upscale gourmet shop, not the kind from the supermarket).

18 thin (⅛-inch-thick)
   baguette slices
1 tablespoon extra-virgin olive oil
3 paper-thin slices prosciutto,
   cut into 18 equal pieces
18 thin slices ripe melon,
   peaches, pears, or plums,
   cut to fit the crostini

1. Preheat the oven to 400ºF. Arrange the bread slices on a baking sheet and brush the tops with the oil. Bake until crisp and golden brown, 7 to 10 minutes. Let cool.

2. Fold the prosciutto into loose ruffles to fit onto the crostini (the prosciutto can hang over the sides of the bread, it's fine). Top each with a piece of fruit. Serve.

CHAPTER 4

Soup It Up—
Hot & Cold Comfort Food

Soup is one of my favorite foods because it's comforting, filling, perfect no matter what the weather is like, super easy, and lasts for days. And there are so many different combinations: warm vegetable soups for cold days, chilled purées for hot days, bean soups, chicken soups—is there anything you can't put in a soup?

As I've been traveling more for work and eating out in restaurants, I've actually discovered a secret about soup: It's usually the healthiest thing on the menu! For years, I always thought a salad was the way to go until I started looking up nutritional information. Holy fat and calories! I think salads at home are wonderful, and they probably were a good light choice in restaurants when people ordered them as a starter.

Now when you go out, most salads are served in these gigantic bowls, drenched in fattening dressing, and covered with pieces of pretty much every entrée they serve! My advice if you're in a restaurant is to skip those crazy salad meals. Only go for the small side salads with the dressing on the side. And whatever you do, promise me—promise me—you'll never fall into that endless salad bowl at the Olive Garden (all right, so I named them, but this is a serious warning!). The salad is fine (well, as fine as plain old iceberg lettuce can be), but their house dressing packs more than 20 grams of fat!

Surprisingly, the soups are usually better choices—yes, even at the O.G.! They are still served in relatively normal-sized bowls (avoid the bread bowl unless you want to tack an extra five-hundred calories on your order), and even the creamy ones usually aren't that bad. Of course, if you choose a clear broth, vegetable soup, or low-fat option, you can't go wrong.

It's well worth the small amount of time and effort it takes to make home-made soup, not just because it tastes a million times better than canned soup, but also because it's much healthier. Canned soups have preservatives and additives and lots and lots of extra salt.

Here are some of my favorite soups, including a healthy take on traditional Italian Wedding Soup.

Rustic Lentil Soup

Makes 10 to 12 servings

This makes a HUGE amount of soup, so use your biggest pot. (You can always freeze some of it for another meal.) This is super-easy and super-quick and because I add little pasta shells to scoop up the extra juice, it can actually make a whole meal. It tastes even better the next day, although it will thicken in your fridge into a not-so-pretty sludge. Just thin it with some extra water when heating it up.

1 pound lentils

1 tablespoon extra-virgin olive oil

1 large onion, diced

3 large carrots, diced

2 large celery ribs, diced

2 garlic cloves, chopped

3 ripe plum (Roma) tomatoes, seeded and diced, or 1 cup drained canned plum tomatoes, broken up

1½ teaspoons dried oregano

3 dried or fresh bay leaves

2 cups small shell pasta

Salt and freshly ground pepper

1. Put the lentils in a colander. Rinse under cold water and sort through to discard any stones or other things you don't want in your soup. Drain and set aside.

2. Heat the oil in a large soup pot over medium heat. Add the onion, carrots, celery, and garlic and cover. Cook, stirring occasionally, until the vegetables soften, about 6 minutes. Add the lentils, tomatoes, oregano, and bay leaves. Pour in 2½ quarts of water. Bring to a boil over high heat. Reduce the heat to medium-low and cook, uncovered, stirring occasionally, until the lentils are almost tender, about 30 minutes.

3. Stir in the pasta and 3 cups of water, and return to a boil over high heat. Season with the salt and pepper. Reduce the heat to medium-low and simmer, stirring often, until the pasta is tender, about 15 minutes. (For a thinner soup, add water as desired; for a thicker soup, just let simmer, stirring occasionally.) Remove the bay leaves. Serve hot.

✻ ✻ ✻ Like the Knife ✻ ✻ ✻

Growing up, my parents always told me to "walk a straight line, like the knife!" If you want to speed up your food prep—especially for things you can't use your chopper for, like when you need beautiful ¼-inch rounds of veggies for soup—you might consider taking a knife skills workshop. You can find them at local cooking schools, upscale grocery stores that have cooking demonstration classes, or even gourmet cookware shops like Williams-Sonoma and Sur La Table (a lot of times they're sponsored by knife companies, so they're free!).

When in Rome . . .

I think it's a great saying to tell people to "shape up," and it sounds beautiful in Italian.
Come il coltello { *Like the Knife* } = KOH-may eel koh-TELL-oh

Zuppa di Verdure

Makes 8 servings

Everyone knows Italy for its pasta and wine, but with twenty-five million acres of farmland, we have tons of amazing vegetables, too. This light, flavorful soup is a vegetarian delight with no beans, meat, or pasta. Just you and yummy Mother Nature.

1 tablespoon extra-virgin olive oil

1 medium onion, chopped

2 medium carrots, cut into ¼-inch-thick rounds

2 medium red-skinned potatoes, scrubbed but unpeeled, halved lengthwise, then cut into ¼-inch-thick half-moons

2 medium zucchini, halved lengthwise, then cut into ¼-inch-thick half-moons

2 garlic cloves, minced

6 cups reduced-sodium chicken broth

3 ripe plum (Roma) tomatoes, seeded and cut into ½-inch dice

2 teaspoons chopped fresh thyme

1 teaspoon salt

¼ teaspoon red pepper flakes

½ cup freshly grated Parmigiano-Reggiano or Parmesan cheese, divided, for serving

1. Heat the oil in a soup pot over medium heat. Add the onion, carrots, and potatoes and cover. Cook, stirring often, until the carrots begin to soften, about 8 minutes. Add the zucchini and garlic and cook, stirring occasionally, until the garlic is fragrant, about 2 minutes.

2. Add the broth and bring to a boil over high heat. Reduce the heat to medium-low. Simmer until the potatoes are tender, about 30 minutes. Add the tomatoes, thyme, salt, and red pepper flakes and simmer until the tomatoes are tender, about 5 minutes more.

3. Ladle into soup bowls and serve hot, topping each serving with 1 tablespoon of Parmesan cheese.

Italian Wedding Soup

Makes 8 servings

Italian wedding soup actually has nothing to do with weddings (although it's a popular soup choice at American receptions). It's from a traditional soup in Italy called *minestra maritata*, or "married soup," because the vegetables and meat work so well together. The English translation got a bit confused and it became known as "wedding soup," but whatever you call it, it's delicious anytime, anywhere.

1 tablespoon extra-virgin olive oil

1 medium onion, chopped

2 medium carrots, chopped

8 cups reduced-sodium chicken broth

1 pound ground turkey (7 percent fat)

½ cup Italian-seasoned dried breadcrumbs

¼ cup freshly grated Parmigiano-Reggiano or Parmesan cheese, plus more for serving

2 large eggs, beaten

1 teaspoon salt

½ teaspoon freshly ground black pepper

1 (5-ounce) bag baby spinach

1. Heat the oil in a soup pot over medium heat. Add the onion and carrots and cook, stirring occasionally, until the onion is translucent, about 5 minutes. Add the broth and bring to a boil over high heat.

2. Meanwhile, mix the turkey, breadcrumbs, ¼ cup grated Parmesan cheese, eggs, salt, and pepper together in a large bowl. Rinse your clean hands under cold water. Using about a heaping teaspoon for each, roll the meat mixture into 48 small meatballs. Transfer the meatballs to a baking sheet.

3. Reduce the heat under the broth to medium. One at a time, carefully drop the meatballs into the broth. Let the soup simmer, adjusting the heat as needed, until the meatballs are cooked through, about 20 minutes. Stir in the spinach and let cook until tender, about 3 minutes more.

4. Ladle into bowls and serve hot, with the grated Parmesan cheese passed on the side.

Chilled Cream of Asparagus Soup

Makes 6 servings

Asparagus is one of my favorite vegetables, not just because it tastes great, but because it's sooo good for you. It's packed with vitamins, antioxidants, nutrients, fiber, and even protein. This creamy soup is perfect for lunch, or a warm summer night's dinner.

1 tablespoon extra-virgin olive oil

1 large onion, chopped

2 pounds asparagus spears, woody stems snapped off, spears cut into 1½-inch pieces

4 cups reduced-sodium chicken broth, plus more as needed

2 tablespoons chopped fresh Italian parsley, plus more for serving

½ teaspoon salt

½ teaspoon freshly ground black pepper

½ cup plus 6 tablespoons reduced-fat sour cream

1. Heat the oil in a soup pot over medium heat. Add the onion and cook, stirring occasionally, until translucent, about 5 minutes. Add the asparagus and stir well. Add the broth and bring to a simmer. Reduce the heat to medium-low and continue to simmer until the asparagus is very tender, about 20 minutes. Stir in the 2 tablespoons chopped parsley.

2. In batches, purée the soup mixture in a blender, leaving the lid slightly ajar to let the steam escape. (Or purée right in the pot with an immersion blender.) Transfer to a bowl. Let cool until tepid, about 1 hour. Cover and refrigerate until chilled, at least 2 hours. To speed up the chilling, you can stick the bowl in a larger bowl of iced water and refrigerate.

3. Just before serving, add ½ cup sour cream to the soup and whisk until smooth. Season with salt and pepper. If the chilled soup seems too thick, thin it out with more broth to the desired consistency. Ladle into soup bowls and serve chilled, topping each serving with a tablespoon of sour cream and a sprinkle of chopped fresh parsley.

Calamari and Potato Cacciuco

Makes 6 to 8 servings

Cacciuco [KAH-cho-koh] is a rib-sticking fish soup-stew. This one keeps it simple with two of my favorites: calamari and chunks of potatoes in a spicy tomato broth. The secret to tender calamari is to avoid overcooking.

1 tablespoon extra-virgin olive oil

1 medium onion, chopped

3 large celery ribs with leaves, thinly sliced

3 garlic cloves, chopped

1 (28-ounce) can Italian plum tomatoes with their juices, chopped

1 cup bottled clam juice

2 tablespoons chopped fresh Italian parsley, plus more for serving

1 teaspoon Italian seasoning

½ teaspoon red pepper flakes

2 large red-skinned potatoes, scrubbed but unpeeled, cut into ½-inch dice

1 pound calamari, sacs cut into ½-inch rings, and tentacles cut into bite-sized clusters

1. Heat the oil in a soup pot over medium heat. Add the onion, celery, and garlic and cook, stirring occasionally, until the onion is translucent, about 5 minutes. Add the tomatoes with their juices, the clam juice, 2 tablespoons chopped parsley, Italian seasoning, and red pepper flakes and bring to a simmer. Reduce the heat to low and continue to simmer, uncovered, until slightly thickened, about 20 minutes.

2. Meanwhile, put the potatoes in a medium saucepan and add enough lightly salted water just to cover the potatoes. Bring to a boil over high heat. Reduce the heat to low and simmer until the potatoes are tender, about 20 minutes. Drain the potatoes over a bowl, reserving the potato cooking water.

3. Add the potatoes and 2 cups of the potato cooking water to the tomato mixture. Return to a simmer. Add the calamari and cook just until heated through but still tender, about 1 minute.

4. Ladle into soup bowls, sprinkle with parsley, and serve hot.

Stracciatella with Spinach

Makes 6 servings

The Chinese aren't the only cooks who make egg-drop soup. *Stracciatella* [strah-cha-TELL-ah] is the Italian version, from the word *stracciato*, which means "torn apart." If you don't have spinach, you can substitute thawed frozen peas. And you can add cooked chicken to the soup, too.

2 quarts reduced-sodium
   chicken broth
1 (5-ounce) bag baby spinach
2 large eggs
½ cup freshly grated Parmigiano-
   Reggiano or Parmesan cheese
1 tablespoon finely chopped fresh
   Italian parsley

1. Bring the broth to a boil in a soup pot over high heat. Stir in the spinach and cook until wilted, about 3 minutes. Reduce the heat to medium so the broth is simmering.

2. Beat the eggs, Parmesan cheese, and parsley together in a small bowl. Whisking the broth mixture constantly, slowly drizzle the egg mixture into the pot. Let cook until the egg firms up, about 1 minute. Ladle into bowls and serve hot.

CHAPTER 5

Switch It Up—
Low-Fat Italian Classics

Even though most authentic Italian food is healthy, a few gut-busting variations have made their way into our homes and hearts. Somehow flat noodles with green vegetables became four-cheese lasagna. *Pasta al burro*—just noodles lightly coated with butter—morphed into pasta Alfredo—spaghetti almost hidden by a butter-and-cheese paste. Anything drowning in cream sauce and loaded only with carbs—good as it tastes—is not going to be good for you.

But that doesn't mean you have to give up these dishes entirely. I took some favorite Italian American recipes and set out to give them a healthy spin—spaghetti Bolognese, lasagna, chicken Parmesan, even meatballs! There's still plenty of cheese and pasta, but I added the vegetables back, cut back on the high-cholesterol ingredients, and simplified the recipes.

In fact, I think that's another great tip for spotting healthy food: If you can easily make out all the ingredients used on the final plate, it's probably pretty good for you. I can see chicken and peppers and parsley. I can't so easily pick out how many cheeses, creams, and meats high in saturated fat were blended together inside restaurant ravioli.

WHOLE-GRAIN PASTA, TAKE TWO

If you read *Skinny Italian*, you know I'm a huge fan of regular pasta, but whole-grain pasta, not so much. But I'm trying to love it! Whole-grain pasta doesn't cook as quickly, and some brands can be too chewy for me. But my husband, Joe, is a convert. He thinks it's got more substance, and he likes the heavier texture so much, he doesn't really like regular pasta anymore.

Any good marriage takes compromise, so I've given whole-grain pasta another chance. And I'm happy to report that in the past few years, whole-grain pastas have gotten much, much better, not just in taste, but also in texture. But if you're like me, and you're hesitant to make the switch, or you have picky eaters in your house that will wrinkle their noses at not-quite-white spaghetti, here are some tips to get the most whole grain into your life:

Mix & Match

Make half regular pasta and half whole grain. Slowly add more and more whole grain, until that's all you're eating.

Regular and whole-grain pasta do cook at different rates (whole grain takes longer), so when cooking them together, put your whole grain in the pot first, cook it for a few minutes, then add the regular pasta.

Get a Grain Blend

Some pastas are already half-and-half, adding extra whole grains but not as much as a full whole-grain pasta. They taste and cook more like regular pasta, and can be an easy, one-pot bridge to whole-grain goodness.

Avoid Dyes

While there are a few pastas that have vegetables mixed in, the amount of vegetables is so small, it's not worth the extra price or what you lose in taste (just use regular pasta with real vegetables!). While the veggie-enhanced pastas aren't great, they aren't bad for you either. Just make sure it's actual vegetables coloring the pasta and not dye. Most pasta marked "tri-color" is just that—only colored. Artificial dyes might make your pasta look prettier, but they're not good for you. And nothing's prettier than real, colored vegetables on real pasta!

Know How Much Whole Grain

Just because a product says it has "whole grain" or "100% grain" or even "3 times as much fiber!" doesn't mean it has a lot. Regular pasta has 2 grams of fiber per serving. Whole-grain pasta has 6 grams. That's a 4-gram difference. Considering you should eat between 25 and 30 grams of fiber a day, decide how that extra 4 grams fits into your life. For me, I eat a lot of vegetables anyway—one cooked artichoke has 10 grams of fiber, 1 cup of cooked peas has 9 grams—so I don't feel guilty if I have regular pasta because I know I'm getting enough fiber in my other foods (and whole-grain pasta has the same amount of fat and just 20 fewer calories than regular pasta). But if you're not getting enough fiber, every little extra bit can help.

Skinny Spaghetti Bolognese

Makes 6 servings

Spaghetti Bolognese can easily go over the top on calorie and fat content when too much and too-fatty meat is added. This version highlights the vegetables that give the sauce such a great flavor, and uses yummy turkey sausage.

1 tablespoon extra-virgin olive oil

1 medium onion, chopped

1 medium carrot, cut into
   ¼-inch dice

1 medium celery rib with leaves,
   cut into ¼-inch dice

1 garlic clove, minced

½ pound sweet or hot Italian
   turkey sausage (about 2 links,
   depending on the brand),
   casings removed

1 (15-ounce) can tomato sauce

1 (6-ounce) can tomato paste

1 cup dry white wine,
   like Pinot Grigio

¼ cup coarsely chopped
   fresh basil

1 pound whole-wheat spaghetti

6 tablespoons freshly grated
   Parmigiano-Reggiano or
   Parmesan cheese for serving

1. To make the sauce, heat the oil in a large saucepan over medium heat. Add the onion, carrot, celery, and garlic. Cook, stirring occasionally until the onion is translucent, about 5 minutes. Add the turkey sausage and cook, occasionally stirring and breaking up the meat well with a wooden spoon, until it loses its raw look, about 8 minutes.

2. Stir in the tomato sauce, tomato paste, wine, and 1 cup water. Bring to a boil. Reduce the heat to medium-low and simmer, stirring occasionally, until the sauce is slightly thickened, at least 30 minutes and up to 2 hours. If the sauce is too thick or threatens to stick to the pan, stir in ¼ cup or so more water. During the last few minutes, stir in the basil.

3. Meanwhile, or when ready to serve, bring a large pot of lightly salted water to a boil over high heat. Add the spaghetti and cook according to the package directions until al dente. Drain well and return to the pot.

4. Add the sauce to the spaghetti and mix well. Divide among 6 pasta bowls, top each with 1 tablespoon of Parmesan cheese, and serve hot.

Veal and Peppers

Makes 6 servings

My family love, love, loves veal and peppers, but it can be easy to eat too much meat. Even though veal shoulder is relatively lean, you're better off using meat as a flavoring and vegetables for the bulk of your meal. This is a great example of how to stretch a small amount of meat with lots of veggies for a quick, healthy, inexpensive meal.

2 tablespoons extra-virgin
    olive oil, divided

1½ pounds boneless veal shoulder,
    cut into 1-inch chunks

¾ teaspoon salt

¼ teaspoon freshly ground
    black pepper

2 medium onions, cut into
    ½-inch-thick half-moons

1 red bell pepper, cored, seeded,
    and cut into ½-inch-wide strips

1 green bell pepper, cored, seeded,
    and cut into ½-inch-wide strips

1 yellow bell pepper,
    cored, seeded, and cut into
    ½-inch-wide strips

2 garlic cloves, minced

2 (8-ounce) cans tomato sauce

2 tablespoons chopped fresh
    oregano or Italian parsley

1. Heat 1 tablespoon of the oil in a large Dutch oven or flameproof casserole over medium-high heat. Season the veal with the salt and pepper. In batches, add the veal and cook, turning occasionally, until lightly browned, about 5 minutes. Transfer to a plate.

2. Add the remaining 1 tablespoon oil to the Dutch oven and heat. Add the onions, the red, green, and yellow peppers, and garlic and cover. Cook, stirring often with a wooden spoon to dislodge the browned bits in the bottom of the pot, until the peppers soften, about 10 minutes.

3. Return the veal to the pot. Stir in the tomato sauce and 1 cup water and bring to a simmer. Cover and cook, stirring occasionally, until the veal is tender, about 1 hour. During the last few minutes, stir in the oregano. Serve hot.

Turkey Meatballs

Makes 4 servings, 12 meatballs

There are millions of ways to make them with millions of different ingredient combinations. My only rule is, they must have sauce! This is my favorite heart-healthy recipe. Meatballs are great to have around because they can do more than get mixed up with spaghetti. Serve them on rolls as a sandwich, with or without mozzarella, provolone, or Parmesan. Slice them up for a pizza topping. Spoon them over polenta or rice. Or eat them right out of a bowl. It's worth making a double batch and freezing half for another meal.

Turkey Meatballs:
Nonstick olive oil spray
1 pound ground turkey (not ground turkey breast)
½ cup Italian-seasoned dried breadcrumbs
½ cup low-fat milk
1 large egg, beaten
3 tablespoons finely chopped fresh Italian parsley
2 garlic cloves, finely chopped
¾ teaspoon salt
¼ teaspoon freshly ground black pepper

The Quickie Tomato Sauce:
1 tablespoon extra-virgin olive oil
1 can (28-ounce) Italian plum tomatoes with their juices, chopped
¼ cup tomato paste
2 tablespoons chopped fresh basil

1. Position a rack in the center of the oven and preheat the oven to 400ºF. Spray a rimmed baking sheet with the nonstick spray.

2. For the meatballs, mix all of the ingredients together in a large bowl. Using clean hands rinsed under cold water, shape the mixture into 12 equal-sized balls, and place on the prepared baking sheet. Bake until the meatballs are lightly browned, about 25 minutes.

3. To make the sauce, heat the oil in a medium saucepan over medium heat. Add the tomatoes and their juices and the tomato paste. Bring just to a boil. Reduce the heat to medium-low and stir in the basil. Simmer to blend the flavors, about 10 minutes. Reduce the heat to very low to keep warm while the meatballs are baking.

4. Add the meatballs to the tomato sauce. Simmer to blend the flavors for about 15 minutes. Serve hot. (The meatballs and sauce can be cooled, covered, and refrigerated for up to 2 days. Or transfer the cooled meatballs and sauce to a covered freezer-proof container and freeze for up to 1 month. Thaw in the microwave oven on medium heat until heated through, about 30 minutes.)

Lasagna Rustica

Makes 9 servings

Is there anything more delicious than layers of pasta, sauce, meat, and cheese? This luscious lasagna includes a good amount of healthy spinach, eggs, and turkey sausage, but you could easily leave out the sausage to make this totally vegetarian. I use no-boil lasagna noodles to save time.

Lasagna Sauce:
1 tablespoon extra-virgin olive oil
1 (28-ounce) can Italian plum tomatoes with their juices, chopped
3 (8-ounce) cans tomato sauce
2 teaspoons dried oregano

1 pound sweet Italian turkey sausage, casings removed
3 (10-ounce) packages thawed frozen chopped spinach, squeezed dry
1 (15-ounce) container reduced-fat ricotta cheese (about 2 cups)
1 large egg plus 1 large egg white
1/4 teaspoon salt
1/4 teaspoon freshly ground black pepper
1 (9-ounce) package dried no-boil flat lasagna noodles
1 (8-ounce) package shredded reduced-fat mozzarella cheese (about 2 cups)
1/4 cup freshly grated Parmigiano-Reggiano or Parmesan cheese

1. Position a rack in the center of the oven. Lightly oil a 13 x 9-inch baking dish.

2. To make the sauce, heat the oil in a large saucepan over medium heat. Add the tomatoes and their juice, the tomato sauce, and oregano and bring just to a simmer. Reduce the heat to low and simmer, stirring often, until slightly thickened, about 20 minutes.

3. Meanwhile, cook the sausage in a large nonstick skillet over medium heat, stirring often and breaking up the meat well with the side of a wooden spoon, until lightly browned, about 10 minutes. Set aside.

4. Mix the spinach and ricotta with the egg and egg white in a medium bowl until combined. Season with the salt and pepper.

5. Spread 1 cup of the tomato sauce in the prepared baking dish. Top with 4 slightly overlapping lasagna sheets. Top with one-third of the spinach-ricotta mixture, spreading to cover evenly, half of the turkey sausage, 1 cup of the mozzarella, and 1 cup sauce, distributing the ingredients as evenly as possible. Top with 4 more sheets of the pasta, another third of the spinach-ricotta mixture, and 1 1/2 cups of sauce. Top with 4 more sheets of the pasta, the remaining spinach-ricotta mixture and turkey sausage, and 1 cup of sauce.

Top with 4 more sheets of the pasta, then the remaining sauce, spreading it evenly to the sides of the dish, and the remaining 1 cup mozzarella. Sprinkle with the Parmesan cheese.

6. Loosely cover the baking dish with aluminum foil, tenting to avoid touching the cheese topping. Bake until bubbling, 50 to 60 minutes. Uncover and cook until cheese is entirely melted, 5 to 10 minutes. Let stand for 15 minutes. Cut the lasagna into 9 portions and serve hot.

✳ ✳ ✳ Cheese, Glorious Cheese ✳ ✳ ✳

You might have noticed I sometimes call for reduced-fat versions of mozzarella and ricotta cheeses, but never Parmesan. That's because there's really no such thing as reduced-fat Parmesan, at least not the true cheese. Parmigiano-Reggiano is so prized in Italy that the name is trademarked, there are strict rules for how it must be made, and truckloads of it have been hijacked at gunpoint. If you can find it in your local grocery or specialty store, buy it! Parmesan cheese is a close cousin and will do fine, as long as you are buying it in blocks and grating it yourself.

Parmigiano-Reggiano is a hard, crumbly cheese that's naturally low-fat already—it has just 1 gram of fat per tablespoon—and packed with calcium. It also has a lot of great protein, the kind that your body can digest in just 45 minutes compared to 4 hours for protein from meat. Because a little amount packs a punch of flavor and nutrients, athletes eat it after they work out, and parents in Italy often sprinkle it over their baby's food.

If you see reduced-fat Parmesan cheese, you're looking at a bag (or, dear Lord, a can) of shredded or grated. It's not going to be fresh, it's not going to be pure, and it's not going to really save you from anything except a great meal.

Faux Fettuccine Alfredo with Broccoli

Makes 6 servings

I don't want to only pick on the Olive Garden. Many other Italian American chain restaurants are just as bad. Take Macaroni Grill for instance. Order their fettuccine Alfredo and you'll go home with 33 grams of saturated fat. Cheesecake that's 800 calories a slice? It's just ridiculous! Delicious food, even those dishes only "inspired" by Italy like fettuccine Alfredo, do not have to be so unhealthy. Here's delicious proof!

1 head broccoli, cut into
   bite-sized florets
1 pound fettuccine pasta
1 tablespoon extra-virgin olive oil
2 garlic cloves, minced
2 tablespoons all-purpose flour
2 cups 2% reduced-fat milk
2 ounces reduced-fat (light)
   cream cheese, softened to
   room temperature
1/2 cup (2 ounces) freshly grated
   Parmigiano-Reggiano or
   Parmesan cheese
1/4 teaspoon salt
1/4 teaspoon freshly ground
   black pepper

1. Bring a large pot of lightly salted water to a boil over high heat. Add the broccoli and cook until barely tender, about 5 minutes. Using a wire sieve, scoop the broccoli out of the water and transfer to a bowl. Set aside.

2. Add the pasta to the water and cook according to the package directions until al dente.

3. Meanwhile, make the sauce, which you want to be finished about the time that the pasta is cooked. Heat the oil and garlic together in a medium saucepan over medium heat just until the garlic is softened, about 1 minute. Put the flour in a bowl, and gradually whisk in the milk. Pour the milk mixture into the saucepan and bring to a simmer, whisking often. Reduce the heat to medium-low and simmer until all raw flour taste is gone, about 1 minute. Remove from the heat, add the cream and Parmigiano cheeses, and whisk until smooth. Season the sauce with the salt and pepper.

4. Drain the pasta and return to its cooking pot. Add the sauce and broccoli and mix well. Transfer to 6 pasta bowls and serve hot.

Stepping Tall

You know those exercise shoes with the rocker bottoms that promise to tone your legs and shape your backside because they have you walking on a weird, high sole? Yeah, Tina Turner and I have known about those for years. We call them "high heels."

One of the reasons European women look so amazing is they walk everywhere and they do it in high heels. I know high heels aren't recommended for all-day, everyday use by foot doctors (although I'm aiming to be buried in mine), any shoe that causes you to concentrate on your balance and use muscles you don't normally use is going to burn more calories. The exercise shoes do work for two simple reasons: 1) Anytime you exercise your body's biggest muscles—your legs and your butt—you're going to burn more calories and fat everywhere, and 2) People who pay $100 for fancy tennis shoes are probably going to use them more.

You can reap the same benefits without the fancy shoes by just making walking a conscious, active part of your daily life. Park farther away from the store entrance. Skip the elevator and take the stairs. Look for reasons to walk. It's the easiest way to get exercise, and it really does do a body good. A recent Harvard study showed that women who walked just three hours a week could cut their risk of heart disease by 40 percent.

Naked Chicken Parmesan

Makes 4 servings

I wanted to return to what makes this dish so special: the Parmesan cheese. Instead of getting lost in the fried breadcrumb crust, the sharp, tangy cheese is the star. To really appreciate it though, you must start with a block of Parmesan (or Parmigiano-Reggiano) cheese and grate it yourself. The bags of pre-grated cheese, or—*Madonna mia!*—the green cans of the powdery stuff, are nowhere near worthy substitutes.

2 teaspoons extra-virgin olive oil

4 boneless, skinless chicken breasts (about 1½ pounds)

½ teaspoon salt

¼ teaspoon freshly ground black pepper

3½ cups The Quickie Tomato Sauce (page 78)

½ cup (2 ounces) shredded reduced-fat mozzarella cheese

¼ cup (1 ounce) freshly grated Parmigiano-Reggiano or Parmesan cheese

1. Preheat the oven to 350ºF.

2. Heat 2 teaspoons olive oil in a large nonstick skillet over medium heat. Season the chicken with the salt and pepper. Add the chicken to the skillet and cook until the undersides are browned, about 3 minutes. Flip the chicken over and brown the other sides, about 3 minutes more. Transfer to a plate.

3. Pour the sauce into a 13 x 9-inch baking dish. Arrange the chicken breasts over the sauce in the dish. Sprinkle 2 tablespoons of mozzarella and 1 tablespoon of Parmesan over each chicken breast. Bake until the cheese is melted and the chicken is cooked through, 15 to 20 minutes. Transfer each portion of chicken to a dinner plate and spoon the sauce around the chicken.

CHAPTER 6

Step It Up—
Gourmet Entrées

ven though most of us are usually in a hurry all day, every day, and need things done as quickly as possible, we don't always want dinner to look like we just threw it together in ten minutes. Sometimes you want to serve an elegant meal, especially when you're having company over. Preparing elaborate, gourmet dishes doesn't have to take two hours. Here are some of my favorite recipes that will impress your guests, but still leave you plenty of time for the thousand other things you need to do.

Don't let the word "gourmet" intimidate you, even if you're a relative virgin in the kitchen. While it has a fancy, almost snobby connotation today, the word actually has humble roots. It comes from the Old French word *gormand*, which means a "glutton" or a big pig, and *gromet,* a serving boy. So if anyone tries to throw the word around to prove their culinary superiority, you can deliver the smack-down and remind them it means greedy little servant boy.

> ### When in Rome . . .
>
> A few Italian phrases that are generally just good
> to have at your disposal:
>
> Magnifico {*Great*} = mag-NEE-fee-koh
> Basta {*That's enough*} = bah-STAH
> ¿Sei pazzo? {*Are you crazy?*} = say PATZ-zoh
> Mi scusi {*Excuse me*} = mee SKOO-zee
> ¿Mi dica? {*Can I help you?*} = mee DEE-kah

Step It Up—Gourmet Entrées

87

Shrimp Scampi

Makes 4 servings

With just two steps, this recipe couldn't be simpler. With the buttery, garlicky sauce, it couldn't seem more indulgent. Serve with something light that will soak up the sauce, like angel hair pasta or Easy Risi e Bisi (see page 118).

1 tablespoon extra-virgin olive oil

2 garlic cloves, thinly sliced

1½ pounds (21/25 count) large shrimp, peeled and deveined

¼ teaspoon salt

¾ cup dry white wine

3 tablespoons freshly squeezed lemon juice

2 tablespoons finely chopped fresh oregano, basil, or Italian parsley

⅛ teaspoon red pepper flakes

3 tablespoons cold unsalted butter, cut into ½-inch cubes

1. Heat the oil and garlic together in a large skillet over medium heat until the garlic begins to color, about 1 minute. Season the shrimp with the salt. Add the shrimp to the skillet and cook, stirring occasionally, until the shrimp turns opaque around the edges, about 3 minutes.

2. Add the wine, lemon juice, oregano, and red pepper flakes and bring to a boil. Cook until the shrimp is opaque in the center, about 1 minute more. Remove the pan from the heat. Add the butter and stir, shaking the pan by its handle, until the butter is melted. Serve hot.

Veal Scaloppine

Makes 4 servings

Any recipe with *scaloppina* (the singular) or *scaloppini/scaloppine* (the plural) in the title means it's made using thin slices or "scallops" of meat. Whether you use veal or chicken, make sure to give it a good pounding, as that will help the meat tenderize and cook faster. I like to serve this with orzo and a green vegetable, like zucchini.

1¼ pounds sliced veal cutlets

½ teaspoon salt

½ teaspoon freshly ground black pepper

3 tablespoons extra-virgin olive oil, divided

¼ cup all-purpose flour

10 ounces cremini (baby bella) mushrooms, thinly sliced

3 tablespoons finely chopped shallots

½ cup dry Marsala, dry sherry, or dry white wine

2/3 cup reduced-sodium beef or chicken broth

2 tablespoons finely chopped fresh Italian parsley

1. One at a time, place a veal cutlet between 2 plastic storage bags. Using a flat meat pounder or a rolling pin, pound the veal until it is about ¼-inch thick. Season with the salt and pepper. Cut the veal into a total of 16 somewhat equal pieces.

2. Heat 2 teaspoons of the oil in a large nonstick skillet over medium-high heat. In batches, dip one-third of the veal in the flour and shake off the excess flour. Add to the skillet and cook, turning occasionally, until lightly browned, about 3 minutes. Transfer to a plate. Repeat twice, using 2 teaspoons of oil, another third of the veal, and the remaining flour each time.

3. Add the remaining tablespoon of oil to the skillet and heat on medium-high. Add the mushrooms and cook, stirring occasionally, until the liquid evaporates and the mushrooms are beginning to brown, about 8 minutes. Add the shallots and cook until softened, about 1 minute.

4. Add the Marsala and bring to a boil. Stir in the broth. Return the veal and any juices on the plate to the skillet. Return to a boil, turning the veal in the sauce, and cook until lightly thickened, about 1 minute. Sprinkle with the parsley and serve hot.

When in Rome . . .

Scaloppine = skal-oh-PEEN-nay

Tagliatelle alla Boscaiola

Makes 6 servings

I'm a huge fan of tagliatelle, and this is one of my all-time favorite recipes. In Italian, *boscaiola* [boose-KAI-oh-la] means "like the woodsman." I've never met an actual "woodsman," but I'm guessing they eat lots of mushrooms since they live in the woods and all.

1 ounce dried porcini mushrooms (about 1 loosely packed cup), quickly rinsed under cold running water to remove surface grit

2 cups boiling water

1 tablespoon extra-virgin olive oil

1 medium onion, chopped

10 ounces cremini (baby bella) mushrooms, thinly sliced

1 garlic clove, minced

1 pound tagliatelle or whole-wheat fettuccine pasta

2 ounces reduced-fat cream cheese

2 tablespoons finely chopped fresh Italian parsley

1/2 teaspoon salt

1/4 teaspoon freshly ground black pepper

1. Bring a large pot of lightly salted water to a boil over high heat.

2. Put the dried mushrooms in a heatproof bowl and cover with the 2 cups boiling water. Let the mushrooms soak, stirring often, until pliable, about 10 minutes. Drain in a wire sieve set over a bowl, reserving the soaking liquid. Coarsely chop the soaked mushrooms. Strain the soaking liquid into a glass measuring cup, but this time leaving behind any grit in the bottom of the bowl.

3. While the mushrooms are soaking, heat the oil in a large skillet over medium heat. Add the onion and cook, stirring occasionally, until softened, about 3 minutes. Add the fresh mushrooms and cook, stirring occasionally, until the mushrooms begin to brown, about 8 minutes. Stir in the garlic and cook until fragrant, about 1 minute. Add the soaked mushrooms and 1/2 cup of the reserved soaking liquid and cook until the liquid reduces to 2 tablespoons or so, about 3 minutes. Remove from the heat and cover.

4. Add the tagliatelle to the pot of boiling water and cook according to the package directions until al dente. Drain in a colander. Return the pasta to its cooking pot.

5. Reheat the remaining mushroom soaking liquid in a microwave oven or small saucepan until simmering. Add the mushroom mixture, cream cheese, parsley, salt, and pepper to the tagliatelle in the pot. Stir well, adding enough of the hot mushroom liquid to make a creamy sauce. Divide among 6 pasta bowls and serve hot.

Pollo Involtini

Makes 4 servings

If you pound your chicken out thin, and place the rolls seam-side down in the baking pan, these delicious stuffed chicken breasts won't need to be tied or toothpicked. Because they are baked, they are nice and juicy, but they might come out of the oven looking a little pale. To pretty them up on the plate, slice them before serving.

4 boneless, skinless chicken breasts (about 1½ pounds)

½ teaspoon plus ⅛ teaspoon salt, divided

½ teaspoon plus ⅛ teaspoon freshly ground black pepper, divided

1 tablespoon extra-virgin olive oil, plus more for the pan

½ medium onion, finely chopped

1 garlic clove, minced

½ cup coarsely chopped frozen thawed artichoke hearts

1 (packed) cup baby spinach (about 2½ ounces)

1 teaspoon finely chopped fresh sage or rosemary

⅓ cup low-fat ricotta cheese

½ cup reduced-sodium chicken broth

¼ cup dry white wine, such as Pinot Grigio

1. Preheat the oven to 400ºF. Lightly oil an 11½ x 8-inch baking dish.

2. Pound the chicken until it is ¼-inch thick. Season the chicken with ½ teaspoon of salt and ½ teaspoon of pepper.

3. Heat the oil in a large skillet over medium heat. Add the onion and cook, stirring occasionally, until softened, about 3 minutes. Add the garlic and cook until fragrant, about 1 minute. Stir in the artichoke hearts. Stir in the spinach and sage and cook until wilted, about 2 minutes. Drain the spinach mixture well in a wire sieve to remove excess moisture. Transfer to a bowl and stir in the ricotta and remaining ⅛ teaspoon salt and ⅛ teaspoon pepper.

4. Place 1 chicken breast, smooth-side down, on a work surface. Spread one-fourth of the spinach-ricotta mixture in the center of the breast, leaving a 1-inch border on all sides. Fold in the sides, and then roll up from the bottom, like a burrito, to enclose the filling. Place the roll, seam-side down, in the baking dish. Repeat with remaining chicken breasts. Pour the broth and wine over the chicken.

5. Bake until an instant-read thermometer inserted in the center of a breast reads 165ºF, about 20 minutes. Transfer each portion to a dinner plate, and top with a spoonful of the pan juices. Serve hot.

Herb-Crusted Tilapia

Makes 4 servings

I love tilapia because its mildness lets the other flavors shine. And I love this recipe because it couldn't be easier or quicker to make, yet it presents on your table like a masterpiece.

1 cup panko breadcrumbs

1 tablespoon finely chopped fresh
   Italian parsley

1 teaspoon dried rosemary

1 teaspoon dried thyme

½ teaspoon granulated garlic

4 tilapia fillets

2 tablespoons extra-virgin olive oil,
   plus more for the baking dish

½ teaspoon salt

¼ teaspoon freshly ground
   black pepper

1 lemon, cut into wedges

1. Position a rack in the top third of the oven and preheat the oven to 400ºF. Lightly oil a 13 x 9-inch baking pan, or line a cookie sheet with parchment paper.

2. Mix the panko, parsley, rosemary, thyme, and granulated garlic in a small bowl. Brush the fillets on both sides with some of the oil and sprinkle on both sides with the salt and pepper. Arrange the fillets in the pan. Divide the breadcrumb mixture evenly over the tops of the fillets, patting it in place. Drizzle with the remaining oil.

3. Bake until the topping is golden brown and the fish looks opaque when flaked in the center with the tip of a small knife, about 15 minutes. Transfer to dinner plates, add the lemon wedges, and serve hot.

✳ ✳ ✳ Clean Fish ✳ ✳ ✳

There's nothing better than a good, clean fish. My father obsesses about the importance of cleaning whole fish perfectly. He could spend hours doing it! He always says "you have to clean it the right way." I've been cleaning fish since I was eleven years old. If you're buying a whole fish, and you don't know how to properly clean it, let your fish guy do it for you. It really will make a huge difference in your final dish.

Risotto Cacciatore

Makes 4 servings

Risotto is a classic creamy Italian rice dish, and I think you're ready for it. Contrary to what they say on *Top Chef,* making a good risotto isn't hard. It needs some tender loving care, which makes it a hard dish to serve in a busy restaurant, but in your own home, you'll have no problem. Perfect risotto really requires just one thing: twenty minutes of constant stirring—well worth every minute for a divine main course.

6 cups reduced-sodium chicken broth

2 tablespoons extra-virgin olive oil, divided

10 ounces cremini (baby bella) mushrooms, thinly sliced

3 tablespoons finely chopped shallots

2 garlic cloves, minced

1½ cups Arborio (risotto) rice

¾ cup dry white wine, such as Pinot Grigio

2 ripe plum (Roma) tomatoes, seeded and cut into ½-inch dice

¼ cup (1 ounce) freshly grated Parmigiano-Reggiano or Parmesan cheese

¼ teaspoon freshly ground black pepper

2 tablespoons chopped fresh basil, for serving

1. Bring the broth to a simmer in a medium saucepan over high heat. Reduce the heat to very low to keep the broth warm.

2. Heat 1 tablespoon of the oil in a large Dutch oven or heatproof casserole over medium-high heat. Add the mushrooms and cook, stirring occasionally, until lightly browned, about 8 minutes. Stir in the shallots and garlic and cook until fragrant, about 1 minute. Transfer to a bowl and set aside.

3. Heat the remaining tablespoon oil in the Dutch oven over medium heat. Add the rice and stir well. Add the wine and stir until almost all of it has been absorbed into the rice, about 1 minute. Ladle in about ¾ cup of the hot broth. Stir constantly, adjusting the heat as necessary so the rice cooks at a steady simmer without boiling, until almost all of the broth has been absorbed, about 2 minutes. Repeat, stirring in another ¾ cup of broth. Continue, adding broth and stirring almost constantly, until the rice is barely tender, about 20 minutes. Add the mushroom mixture and tomatoes and cook, stirring just once or twice to avoid breaking the tomatoes, just until the tomatoes are heated through, about 1 minute. Add another ¾ cup of broth and stir until the rice is tender, about 1 minute. If you run out of broth before the rice is tender, use hot water.

4. Stir in the Parmesan. Season with the pepper. Add enough broth or hot water to give the risotto a loose, but not soupy, consistency. Divide among 4 pasta bowls. Sprinkle with the basil and serve hot.

✳ ✳ ✳ **Pasta or Not?** ✳ ✳ ✳

Although they have similar consistencies, especially when soaked in broth or cream sauce, not every little yellow thing on the Italian plate is a pasta. Here's a primer:

- Risotto = Not pasta, it's rice.
- Orzo = Yes pasta, although it's confusingly shaped like rice.
- Polenta = Neither; it's a cooked dough made from cornmeal.
- Pastine/Peperini/Stellini = Yes pasta, tiny shapes for soups.

CHAPTER 7

Grill It Up—
Sizzling Selections

I don't know if it's an Italian thing or a Jersey thing, but I love cooking over an open flame. There's something so primitive and natural about it. For all the fancy gas cooktops they make now, nothing compares to how something tastes (and smells!) hot off the grill.

All the men in my family love to light up the grill, but even my mom can sizzle a steak like nobody's business. Anybody can master the fine art of grilling; it's all about taming the flame.

When you cook on top of the stove, do you cook everything over high heat? Or when you bake, do you put the oven temperature to 500ºF? Of course not, because most food would burn. So, why is that when most people grill, they cook the food over high heat—a sure-fire way to overcook their dinner?

Whether you use a gas or a charcoal grill, you need to watch your heat. With a gas grill, it's easy: Just adjust the heat with the turn of the thermostat. High heat is about 500ºF, and medium is around 375ºF (you want to use medium). With a charcoal grill, just let the coals burn to the right temperature. If you can only hold your hand just above the cooking grate for 1 to 2 seconds, then it is too hot. For medium heat, let the coals burn down for about 15 minutes or so, and check again. You should be able to hold your hand above the grate for 3 seconds.

A couple of quick tips from my backyard to yours to up your grilling game:

- **Always cook with the grill lid closed.** This cuts down on the oxygen which fuels the fire, and will help keep flare-ups under control. You probably won't have a lot of flare-ups with these recipes because I've cut back on the oil. Dripping oil, as well as fat from meats and poultry skin, is what causes most flare-ups.

- **Grill on a clean grate.** It amazes me that people keep their stovetops clean but let old food pieces pile up on their grill. Something black and crusty from last month's BBQ sticking to your delicious new food will not be pretty. You can brush a hot grill before you put on new food, but it's easiest to clean the grate after you grill every single time. After the new food is removed and been eaten, but while the grate is still warm, use a stiff wire brush and a little elbow grease.

- **Oil the food, not the cooking grate.** This helps keep the food, especially seafood, from sticking.

- **Trim the fat before you grill.** Just cutting off the fatty edges you can see on a piece of meat can remove up to 75 percent of the saturated fat.

Chicken Spiedini

Makes 4 servings

Spiedini [spee-ah-DEEN-ee] means "skewers" in Italian, and it's our version of grilled kebabs. What sets them apart is the breadcrumb crust and Italian herbs. For color, you can add a cherry tomato to the top of the skewer after you take it off the grill. The most important thing is to make sure the heat isn't too high, or the crumbs will brown before the chicken is cooked through.

1/3 cup Italian-seasoned dry breadcrumbs

2 tablespoons freshly grated Parmesan or Romano cheese

2 (8-ounce) boneless, skinless chicken halves, cut into 16 pieces, each about 1-inch square

2 tablespoons extra-virgin olive oil

1/2 large red bell pepper, cored, seeded, and cut into 8 pieces, each about 1-inch square

1/2 large green bell pepper, cored, seeded, and cut into 8 pieces, each about 1-inch square

1/2 medium-sized sweet onion, cut in half again, separated into 8 pieces, each with 2 or 3 layers of onion

2 tablespoons finely chopped fresh basil or Italian parsley

1. Prepare a grill for medium cooking over direct heat.

2. Mix the breadcrumbs and Parmesan cheese in a shallow bowl. Lightly brush the chicken pieces with some of the oil. Roll the chicken in the breadcrumb mixture to coat. For each spiedini, thread 4 chicken pieces, alternating with 2 red pepper pieces, 2 green pepper pieces, and 2 onion pieces, onto metal skewers. (If you use wooden skewers, soak them first in cold water to cover for 30 minutes, then drain.) Do not pack the ingredients closely together, but leave a little space between them. Brush the vegetables with the remaining oil.

3. Make sure the grilling grate is clean. Place on the grill and cover with the grill lid. Grill, with the lid closed as much as possible, turning occasionally, until the chicken is opaque when pierced at the center with the tip of a sharp knife and the crumbs are browned, about 8 minutes. Transfer to a platter, sprinkle with the basil, and serve.

Rosemary Shrimp Skewers

Makes 4 servings

When you're reducing the fat, salt, and sugar in your diet, other flavors can step in and make your meals magic. Rosemary is a fantastic herb because it's fragrant and super healthy, adding fiber, iron, calcium, and amino acids to your food. It's also believed to help improve memory and concentration. Paired with omega-3-rich shrimp, rosemary is great for your brain and your body!

2 tablespoons extra-virgin olive oil

1 tablespoon freshly squeezed lemon juice

3 garlic cloves, minced

2 teaspoons finely chopped fresh rosemary

1 teaspoon dried oregano

¼ teaspoon salt

¼ teaspoon freshly ground black pepper

24 large (21/25 count) shrimp, peeled and deveined, with tail segment left attached

Lemon wedges, for serving

1. Prepare a grill for direct cooking over medium heat.

2. Mix the oil, lemon juice, garlic, rosemary, oregano, salt, and pepper in a medium bowl. Add the shrimp and toss well to coat. Cover and refrigerate for 15 to 30 minutes, but no longer.

3. Remove the shrimp from the marinade, letting it cling to the shrimp. For each serving, thread 6 shrimp, keeping each one in its natural "C" shape, onto a metal skewer. (If using wooden skewers, soak in cold water for 30 minutes.)

4. Place the shrimp on the grill and cover with the grill lid. Grill, with the lid closed as much as possible, turning occasionally, until the shrimp are opaque, about 5 minutes. Serve hot, with the lemon wedges.

Note: If you want to use actual rosemary skewers: Cut four 12-inch lengths of sturdy rosemary branches. Strip off all but the top 3 inches of the leaves. Soak the rosemary branches in cold water for 30 minutes. Skewer the shrimp first on metal skewers to make holes in the shrimp. Remove the metal skewer and thread the shrimp through the holes onto the rosemary branches. Cover the exposed rosemary leaves on each branch with a piece of aluminum foil. Grill as directed. Remove the foil and serve the shrimp on their fragrant rosemary skewers.

Grilled Tuna with Asparagus

Makes 4 servings

Tuna is very lean and can dry out very quickly when it's overcooked (that's why so many people eat it raw). This is my exception to the don't-grill-over-high-heat rule. You don't want to *always* grill over high heat, but in the case of a tuna steak, it's perfect because it sears the outside quickly, keeping the inside moist.

3 tablespoons extra-virgin olive oil, divided
4 garlic cloves, halved
1 medium onion, finely chopped
1 ripe plum tomato, seeded and cut into 1/2-inch dice
1 tablespoon finely chopped fresh oregano
3/4 teaspoon salt, divided
1/2 teaspoon freshly ground black pepper, divided
4 (6-ounce) tuna steaks
1 pound thin asparagus, woody stems snapped off
Lemon wedges for serving

1. Prepare a grill for direct cooking over high heat.

2. Heat 1 tablespoon of oil with the garlic in a medium skillet over medium heat until the garlic begins to color, about 1 minute. Add the onion and cook, stirring occasionally, until the onion is translucent, about 5 minutes. Stir in the tomato and oregano and cook until the tomato is heated through, about 1 minute. Season with 1/4 teaspoon of salt and 1/4 teaspoon of pepper. Set aside.

3. Brush the tuna on both sides with 1 tablespoon of oil, and season with 1/4 teaspoon salt and the remaining 1/4 teaspoon pepper.

4. Toss the asparagus with the remaining tablespoon of oil in a large bowl. Place the tuna on the grill. Lay the asparagus on the grill, perpendicular to the grid. Cover with the lid. Grill, until the undersides are seared with grill marks, about 2 1/2 minutes. Flip the tuna over and roll the asparagus to its other side. Cover and grill until the tuna is medium-rare (pierce in the center with the tip of a small sharp knife to check) and the asparagus is crisp-tender, about 2 1/2 minutes more. If the tuna is done before the asparagus (or vice versa), just remove it to a platter and tent with aluminum foil to keep warm.

5. Transfer the asparagus to a platter and season with the remaining 1/4 teaspoon salt. Top with the tuna. Spoon the warm onion mixture over each tuna steak, add the lemon wedges, and serve hot.

Steak Salad with Light Balsamic Vinaigrette

Makes 4 servings

This is the perfect example of how to use meat as a flavoring with vegetables as the main component of your dish. The marinated steak is amazing hot off the grill, and even better the next day. I could eat this salad every day, so I usually throw an extra steak on the grill to make sure I have leftovers.

½ cup balsamic vinegar

1 teaspoon Dijon mustard

2 garlic cloves, minced

½ teaspoon salt

¼ teaspoon freshly ground black pepper

3 tablespoons extra-virgin olive oil

2 New York strip steaks (about 12 ounces each and ½-inch thick)

2 romaine hearts, cut into bite-sized pieces

1 pint cherry tomatoes, halved

1. To make the dressing, whisk the vinegar, mustard, garlic, salt, and pepper together in a small bowl. Gradually whisk in the oil.

2. Pour about 3 tablespoons of the dressing into a 1-gallon resealable plastic bag. Add the steaks and turn to coat with the dressing. Let stand while the grill is heating. Set the remaining vinaigrette aside.

3. Prepare a grill for direct cooking over medium heat.

4. Remove the steak from the marinade. Place on the grill and cover with the lid. Grill until the undersides are seared with grill marks, about 3 minutes. Flip the steaks, cover, and grill 3 to 4 minutes, until the steak gives slightly when pressed with a fingertip for medium-rare. (125°F to 130°F on an instant-read thermometer.) Remove the steaks from the grill and let stand for 3 to 5 minutes.

5. Whisk the remaining vinaigrette well. Toss the romaine lettuce and cherry tomatoes with the vinaigrette and spread the salad on a large platter. Cut the steaks across the grain into ½-inch-thick slices. Arrange on top of the salad and serve immediately.

✳ ✳ ✳ The Beauty of Balsamic ✳ ✳ ✳

Balsamic vinegar doesn't just taste amazing, it can actually help you get (or stay) skinny—thanks to the pepsin. Pepsin is an enzyme that helps your body break down food. Can your Thousand Island say that?

Zesty Grilled Pork Loin Chops

Makes 6 servings

If you want to eat healthier, one of the first things you need to cut back on drastically is red meat. Yes, steak is delicious, but instead of eating one the size of your face, eat it as a flavoring, like in my Steak Salad with Light Balsamic Vinaigrette (see page 104). But for those days when you want to cut into a chop of something, use pork instead. It's much leaner, still juicy, and will give you the same knife-and-fork satisfaction with a third of the saturated fat.

6 boneless pork loin chops (about 4 ounces each and ½-inch thick)

2 tablespoons extra-virgin olive oil

2 tablespoons chili powder

1 teaspoon fennel seeds, crushed in a mortar or under a heavy skillet

½ teaspoon salt

4 garlic cloves, minced

1. One at a time, place a pork chop between 2 plastic storage bags. Using a flat meat pounder or a rolling pin, pound the chop until it is ¼-inch thick.

2. Brush the chops with the oil. Mix the chili powder, fennel seeds, salt, and garlic together in a small bowl. Sprinkle and rub the spice mixture over both sides of the pork chops. Let stand while the grill is heating.

3. Prepare a grill for direct cooking over medium heat.

4. Make sure the grate is clean. Place the pork chops on the grill and cover with the grill lid. Grill until the undersides are seared with grill marks, about 2½ minutes. Flip the chops, cover, and grill until the other sides are seared and the chops feel firm when pressed with a fingertip, about 2½ minutes more. Remove from the grill. Serve hot.

Grilled Italian Vegetables

Makes 4 servings

This is a great side dish for any recipe, but especially those in this chapter since you've already got the grill fired up. I personally love the black char marks on my veggies—it makes them seem more rustic and authentic, like they grill them up in the countryside in Italy.

1 large red bell pepper

1 tablespoon extra-virgin olive oil

2 garlic cloves, minced

1 medium zucchini, cut on the diagonal into long ½-inch-thick slices

1 medium yellow squash, cut on the diagonal into long ½-inch-thick slices

¼ teaspoon salt

¼ teaspoon freshly ground black pepper

2 tablespoons chopped fresh basil

2 tablespoons toasted pine nuts (see Note)

Note: To toast pine nuts, heat a dry skillet over medium heat. Add the pine nuts and cook, stirring occasionally, until light brown, 2 to 3 minutes. Transfer to a plate and let cool.

1. Prepare a grill for direct cooking over medium heat.

2. Cut the top and bottom off the red pepper to make "lids" and reserve. Remove and discard the stem. Cut the bell pepper lengthwise and open it up into a large strip. Cut out and discard the ribs and seeds.

3. Mix the oil and garlic together in a large bowl. Add the zucchini and yellow squash and stir to coat with the oil mixture.

4. Place the red pepper strip and "lids" on the grill, skin-side down, and cover with the grill lid. Grill until the skin begins to blister, about 5 minutes. Place the zucchini and yellow squash on the grate with the slices perpendicular to the grate so they don't fall through. Grill, with the lid closed as much as possible, occasionally turning the zucchini and squash (but not the red pepper), until they are tender and the red pepper skin is blackened and blistered, about 5 minutes. Transfer the zucchini and yellow squash to a serving bowl, and put the red pepper in its own small bowl.

5. Tent the squash mixture with aluminum foil to keep warm. Let the red pepper cool, uncovered, until easy to handle. Remove the blackened skin, and coarsely chop the red pepper. Add to the squash mixture. Season with salt and pepper. Sprinkle with the basil and pine nuts and serve warm.

Veggie-Stuffed Portobello Mushrooms

Makes 4 servings

I adore portobello mushrooms, and while they are great stuffed with sausage, they're amazing stuffed with veggies and white wine. These are definitely big enough to make a meal. Serve them with a side salad, with some of my Light Balsamic Vinaigrette (see page 104).

2 tablespoons extra-virgin
  olive oil, divided
1 small onion, finely chopped
½ cup (¼-inch) diced red
  bell pepper
1 garlic clove, minced
¼ cup dry white wine
1 (5-ounce) bag baby spinach
2 ounces reduced-fat
  cream cheese
2 tablespoons Italian-seasoned
  breadcrumbs
1 tablespoon chopped fresh basil
  or Italian parsley
¼ teaspoon salt
¼ teaspoon freshly ground
  black pepper
4 large portobello mushroom caps
  (about 3½ ounces each)
2 tablespoons freshly grated
  Parmigiano-Reggiano or
  Parmesan cheese

1. Prepare a grill for direct cooking over medium heat. If using charcoal, leave it heaped in a mound and do not spread to the edges.

2. Heat 1 tablespoon of oil in a large skillet over medium heat. Add the onion, red pepper, and garlic and cook, stirring occasionally, until the onion is tender, about 5 minutes. Add the wine and let it boil until reduced to 2 tablespoons, about 3 minutes. In batches, stir in the spinach and cook until wilted and tender, about 3 minutes. Drain the spinach mixture in a colander and press with a spatula to remove excess moisture. Transfer to a bowl and stir in the cream cheese, breadcrumbs, basil, salt, and pepper.

3. Trim any remaining stems from the mushrooms caps. Brush the mushroom caps with the remaining tablespoon of oil. Place the mushrooms on the grill and cover with the grill lid. Grill until the underside is seared with grill marks, about 2 minutes. Flip the mushrooms, cover, and grill until they begin to give off their juices, about 3 minutes more. Remove from the grill.

4. Divide the filling among the mushroom caps and sprinkle with the Parmesan cheese. For a charcoal grill, place the stuffed mushroom caps around the perimeter of the cooking grate, not directly over the coals. For a gas grill, place the stuffed mushroom caps over a turned-off burner. Grill, with the lid closed, until the stuffing is heated through and the cheese is melted, 12 to 15 minutes. Remove from the grill and serve hot.

CHAPTER 8

Veg It Up—
Vegetarian Meals & Side Dishes

Your mom wasn't kidding when she said to eat your veggies. According to the Centers for Disease Control, people who eat lots of fruits and vegetables have a much lower risk for heart disease, type 2 diabetes, stroke, and even some cancers compared to those who only eat a small amount. They also recommend that you eat a variety of different colors everyday—some green, some red, some orange, yellow, purple, blue . . . you get the idea.

Everyone knows carrots and broccoli are good for you, but here are some of the more traditional Italian vegetables you should add to your diet—and why:

ARTICHOKES

Artichokes are part of the thistle family, and what we eat is actually an undeveloped flower. You knew they were fun to eat, and now you know why—you're eating a big, tender flower! They're also super great for your heart, and have lots of fiber, potassium, calcium, magnesium, folic acid, and vitamin C. Artichokes are also believed to help the liver regenerate itself—a valuable trick if red meat and too much alcohol plays too big a part in your diet.

ASPARAGUS

Asparagus has tons of fiber and folate, iron and even protein, but one of the best endorsements I can give it is that it's also great for anti-aging. It's packed with anti-inflammatory nutrients, antioxidants, and tons of vitamin K, which is believed to prevent osteoporosis, Alzheimer's disease, and other degenerative diseases.

BELL PEPPERS

I love adding bell peppers to my recipes because they add a splash of bright color, and crazy amounts of vitamins A and C (1 cup of peppers has more than twice the amount of vitamin C as an orange). Vitamin C is critical for the body's immune system, but it leaves your body quickly, so you need to get it every day. A single cup of bell peppers will give you 29 percent of the daily recommended calcium intake without any excess fat or sugar.

EGGPLANT

I love everything about eggplants, from their pretty, purple, shiny skin to their spongy texture and zippy taste. They're also considered a brain food thanks to a phytonutrient called nasunin that helps protect brain cell membranes. And tiny compounds in eggplant are antimicrobial, antiviral, and hunt down free radicals that can cause cancer.

ESCAROLE

Escarole has very few calories, lots of fiber, and a huge amount of vitamin A and vitamin K. Vitamin A is great for your skin and helps protect against lung and mouth cancers.

PEAS

Maybe you already know how good peas are for you, but they're one of my favorite vegetables and I throw them in everything, so let's cover them anyway. Green peas are chock-full of vitamins K, C, B-1, and A, but they also have a good dose of manganese, folate, and tryptophan. Tryptophan is an amazing enzyme (one of the ten best, so I'm told) that helps regulate your appetite, helps you sleep better, and is a natural mood enhancer, combating depression and anxiety. Who knew humble peas were Nature's Prozac? (Maybe that's why I'm an optimistic person—I'm addicted to peas!)

SPINACH

If you're looking for the biggest nutritional bang per cup, spinach has it. One cup of boiled spinach will give you 1110 percent of your daily value of vitamin K, 37 percent of vitamin A, and more than 30 percent of your manganese, folate, magnesium, iron, and vitamin C. Spinach's anti-inflammatory properties—excessive inflammation is a cancer risk—make it a superpower against cancer, especially aggressive prostate cancer. While I love to eat fresh spinach in salads, boiling it down will give you six times the volume, and six times the benefits.

ZUCCHINI

Like most squash, zucchini is full of fiber, vitamins C and A, and magnesium, but it's also a great source of manganese and omega-3 fatty acids. Manganese is a goodie; it helps your body's metabolism, enzymes, and glucose tolerance, and helps produce sex hormones (I find that funny considering the shape of zucchini).

Asparagus and Potato Frittata

Makes 6 servings

A frittata is an Italian cross between an omelette and a quiche. It comes from the Italian word *fritto,* "to fry," but don't worry, we're using healthy oil, egg whites, and vitamin-rich asparagus. It's a full meal—perfect for Meatless Mondays or fasting Fridays or any vegetarian day in between.

1 large red-skinned potato (about 6 ounces), scrubbed but unpeeled, halved lengthwise, and then cut into ¼-inch-thick slices

12 ounces asparagus, woody stems snapped off, cut into 1-inch pieces

2 tablepoons extra-virgin olive oil, divided

1 medium onion, finely chopped

2 garlic cloves, minced

4 large eggs plus 2 large egg whites

2 tablespoons freshly grated Parmigiano-Reggiano or Parmesan cheese

½ teaspoon salt

¼ teaspoon freshly ground black pepper

1. Bring a medium pot of lightly salted water to a boil over high heat. Add the potato slices and reduce heat to medium. Simmer until tender, about 8 minutes. Using a wire sieve, scoop the potatoes out of the water and transfer to a bowl. Add the asparagus to the water and turn heat to high. Boil until the asparagus is just tender, about 5 minutes. Drain in a colander and rinse under cold running water. Drain again and pat dry. Add to the potatoes.

2. Heat the oil over medium heat in an ovenproof 10-inch skillet. Add the onions and garlic and cook, until the onion is tender, about 5 minutes. Add to the potato mixture.

3. Position the broiler rack about 8 inches from the source of heat and preheat the broiler on high.

4. Whisk the eggs, whites, cheese, salt, and pepper in a medium bowl. Add the potato mixture. Return the skillet to medium heat. Pour in the egg mixture and spread with a spatula. Cook until the edges begin to set, about 30 seconds. Using the spatula, lift the cooked edges of the frittata, and tilt the frying pan to allow the liquid egg on top to flow underneath. Continue cooking, until the top is almost set, about 4 minutes.

5. Place skillet under the broiler until the frittata puffs and is golden brown, about 1 minute. Slide the frittata out of the skillet onto a plate. Place a serving plate on top of the plate and invert the plate and platter together to turn the frittata over onto the platter. Cut into wedges and serve hot or warm.

Balsamic Green Beans

Makes 8 servings

These are my specialty—one of my most favorite side dishes. I serve them warm for dinner, and cold for lunch. And even though they don't have strings on them anymore, we still call them "string beans" in my house.

2 tablespoons extra-virgin olive oil
2 tablespoons balsamic vinegar
2 garlic cloves, finely chopped
½ teaspoon salt
¼ teaspoon freshly ground
   black pepper
1½ pounds green beans, trimmed,
   cut into 1-inch lengths

1. Bring a large saucepan of lightly salted water to a boil over high heat.

2. Heat the oil, vinegar, garlic, salt, and pepper together in a small saucepan over very low heat, stirring constantly, until the garlic is fragrant, about 3 minutes. Do not let the mixture come to a boil. Remove from the heat and let stand while cooking the green beans.

3. Add the green beans to the boiling water and cook until barely tender, about 5 minutes. Drain in a colander. Transfer to a serving bowl. Drizzle with the balsamic vinegar mixture, toss well, and serve hot.

✳ ✳ ✳ String Green Bean Salad ✳ ✳ ✳

If you have leftover Balsamic Green Beans, you can whip up a quick, delicious, nutritious salad with them. Mix them with a can of tuna, some chopped grape tomatoes, a squeeze of lemon, and a spoonful of low-fat mayo.

Roasted Cauliflower with Garlic and Olives

Makes 6 servings

Even if you have a small family, make the entire batch. Leftovers are amazing heated in the microwave and tossed with pasta, a drizzle of olive oil, and some Parmesan. I'm a huge anchovy lover, so I sometimes also add a 2-ounce can of drained, chopped anchovies to the mix when I stir the olives and lemon juice into the roasting cauliflower.

1 head cauliflower, broken into bite-sized florets

2 tablespoons plus 1 teaspoon extra-virgin olive oil

2 garlic cloves, thinly sliced

½ cup pitted and coarsely chopped kalamata olives

1 tablespoon freshly squeezed lemon juice

½ teaspoon salt

¼ teaspoon freshly ground black pepper

¼ cup (1 ounce) freshly grated Parmigiano-Reggiano or Parmesan cheese

1. Preheat the oven to 450ºF. Lightly oil a large rimmed baking sheet.

2. Toss the cauliflower with 2 tablespoons of oil. Spread in the prepared baking sheet and bake for 10 minutes.

3. Mix the garlic and the remaining teaspoon of oil in a small bowl. Stir into the cauliflower and continue roasting until the cauliflower begins to brown around the edges, about 10 minutes more.

4. Add the olives and lemon juice to the cauliflower in the baking sheet and stir to combine. Season with the salt and pepper. Sprinkle with the Parmesan. Continue to roast until the cheese melts, about 5 minutes more. Transfer to a serving bowl and serve hot.

Easy Risi e Bisi

Makes 6 servings

Made in the classic style, risi e bisi is really risotto without wine but with peas. This version has similar flavors but is much quicker. It uses long-grain rice for fluffy results. If you wish, substitute ¼ cup of dry white wine for an equal amount of the chicken broth.

1 tablespoon extra-virgin olive oil

1 small onion, chopped

1½ cups long-grain rice

3 cups reduced-sodium chicken broth

¼ teaspoon salt

1 cup frozen thawed peas or cooked fresh peas

¼ cup (1 ounce) freshly grated Parmigiano-Reggiano or Parmesan cheese

¼ teaspoon freshly ground black pepper

1. Heat the oil in a medium saucepan over medium heat. Add the onion and cook, stirring occasionally, until the onion is translucent, about 4 minutes. Add the rice and stir well without browning, about 30 seconds. Add the broth and salt and bring to a boil.

2. Reduce the heat to medium-low and cover tightly. Simmer, without stirring, until the rice is tender and has absorbed the broth, about 18 minutes.

3. Add the peas to the saucepan, but do not stir them in. Cover again and let stand for 5 minutes, so the steam in the pan heats the peas.

4. Stir with a fork to combine the peas and fluff the rice. Stir in the Parmesan cheese. Season with the pepper. Serve hot.

Note: You can form leftover risi e bisi into delicious, crispy rice cakes. Add a beaten egg to the cold, thick rice. Grab small scoops and shape into patties. Coat with Italian breadcrumbs. Then sauté in a little olive oil in a skillet over medium heat until crisp on both sides and heated through, about 5 minutes.

✷ ✷ ✷ Royal Rice ✷ ✷ ✷

Risi e bisi is a classic Italian rice-and-peas dish from Venice. It's so special, that in the olden days, the Doge of Venice (what they called the leader of the "Most Serene Republic of Venice" for a thousand years) decreed it could only be made on certain feast days. Thankfully, we can make it any time we want now. It's considered national comfort food, sort of like mac-and-cheese in America, but is much healthier.

Escarole and Beans

Makes 8 servings

If you've never had escarole, this is the place to start! While it starts as a leafy, green lettuce, it cooks down tender and sweet in this creamy dish. It's another recipe that easily makes a lot, and makes for great, time-saving leftovers the next day (turn it into soup by adding broth, chopped tomatoes, and a little prosciutto). Escarole is very sandy, so wash it really well in a couple changes of water before using.

2 heads escarole

2 tablespoons extra-virgin olive oil

1 medium onion, chopped

2 garlic cloves, thickly sliced

2 (15-ounce) cans cannellini beans, with their juices

½ teaspoon salt

¼ teaspoon red pepper flakes

1. Core the escarole and coarsely chop the leaves. In batches, add the escarole to a large bowl of cold water and agitate well to loosen the dirt. Lift the escarole out of the water, leaving the dirt in the bottom of the bowl, and transfer to another bowl. Do not dry the escarole.

2. Bring a large pot of salted water to a boil over high heat. Stir in the escarole and cook for 5 minutes. This removes some of its bitterness. Drain well.

3. Heat the oil in a large saucepan over medium heat. Add the onion and garlic and cook, stirring occasionally, until tender, about 5 minutes. Add the escarole and the undrained beans. Season with the salt. Cover and cook, stirring often, to blend the flavors, about 10 minutes. Stir in the red pepper flakes. Serve hot.

Peperonata

Makes 8 servings

Peperonata is a stew made of peppers and whatever else people could find in their gardens. It's another dish worth making a big batch of, and having in the refrigerator. Serve on crostini, toss with pasta for a quick supper, chop it up and mix it into scrambled eggs, or serve heated on top of fried eggs.

1 tablespoon extra-virgin olive oil

2 medium red-skinned potatoes, scrubbed but unpeeled, cut into ½-inch dice

1 large onion, sliced into ½-inch-thick half-moons

1 medium red bell pepper, cored, seeded, and cut into ½-inch-wide strips

1 medium green bell pepper, cored, seeded, and cut into ½-inch-wide strips

1 medium yellow pepper, cored, seeded, and cut into ½-inch-wide strips

½ cup hearty red wine, such as Shiraz

¼ teaspoon salt

¼ teaspoon red pepper flakes

2 ripe plum (Roma) tomatoes, seeded and cut into ½-inch dice

¼ cup chopped fresh basil

1. Heat the oil in a large nonstick skillet over medium heat. Add the potato and cook, stirring occasionally, until golden brown and beginning to soften, about 5 minutes. Add the onion and cook, stirring occasionally, until softened, about 3 minutes.

2. Add the red, green, and yellow peppers and the wine and stir well. Season with the salt and red pepper flakes. Cover and reduce the heat to medium-low. Simmer until the peppers and potatoes are tender, about 20 minutes.

3. Stir in the tomatoes and cook, uncovered, until they are heated through, about 3 minutes. Stir in the basil. Serve hot, warm, or at room temperature.

Piselli al Prosciutto

Makes 8 servings

When I want to be super quick and just cook with what I have on hand, I use frozen peas, which are delicious. But I do have a soft spot for fresh peas, so feel free to use those as well. Just buy two pounds in their shell, and shell 'em (great mom, girlfriend, or kid-time activity!). Cook the fresh peas in lightly salted boiling water until tender, about 5 minutes. Drain well.

2 tablespoons extra-virgin olive oil

2 ounces thickly sliced prosciutto, cut into ¼-inch dice

1 cup chopped sweet onion, such as Maui or Vidalia

1 pound frozen thawed peas

¼ teaspoon freshly ground black pepper

⅛ teaspoon salt

1. Heat the oil in a medium skillet over medium heat. Add the prosciutto and cook, stirring occasionally, until beginning to brown, about 3 minutes. Add the onion and cook, stirring occasionally, until tender, about 5 minutes.

2. Add the peas and 2 tablespoons water. Cook, stirring often, until the peas are heated through, about 5 minutes. Season with the pepper and salt. Serve hot.

Very Veggie Roast

Makes 6 servings

You need two baking sheets to make this. You want that roasted, caramelized flavor, but if crowded, the veggies will steam and not roast. The veggies will shrink during cooking, but if you try to crowd them into a single pan, you'll end up with mushy veggies. Line the pans with aluminum foil for easy cleanup.

2 tablespoons extra-virgin olive oil, plus more for the pans

2 garlic cloves, minced

1/2 teaspoon salt

1/2 teaspoon freshly ground black pepper

1 medium eggplant (about 1¼ pounds), cut into 1-inch cubes

1 large zucchini, cut into 1-inch chunks

1 large yellow squash, cut into 1-inch chunks

1 large red bell pepper, cored, seeded, and cut into 1-inch squares

1 medium onion, cut into 1-inch chunks

2 tablespoons chopped fresh Italian parsley

1. Position racks in the top third and center of the oven and preheat the oven to 450ºF. Line 2 large rimmed baking sheets with aluminum foil and lightly oil the foil.

2. Mix the 2 tablespoons oil, garlic, salt, and pepper in a very large bowl. Add the eggplant, zucchini, yellow squash, red pepper, and onion and toss, trying to keep the onion intact at this point. Divide the mixture among the baking sheets.

3. Roast for 15 minutes. Stir, separating the onion layers at this point. Continue roasting until the vegetables are tender, about 15 minutes more. Sprinkle with the parsley and serve hot, warm, or at room temperature.

CHAPTER 9

Whip It Up—
Extra Fast Food

As if all my recipes weren't fast enough, here are my *extra* fast foods. Perfect for those nights when you completely forgot you actually have to feed yourself or your family (scary how often that happens when life gets busy!).

While the prep and cooking times are quick, I want to talk to you about how to slow down in the rest of your life. The treadmill is a great place to be in a hurry. Feel free to run up those stairs. But doing everything in a blur all the time is actually hazardous to your health.

Italians are known for simple cooking, and yes, a lot of our recipes are quick, but we don't eat in a hurry. Italian dinners are long, relaxed, drawn-out affairs. We walk around the house talking first, munching on antipasti and wine to get our stomachs started. Then we sit and share our food, share stories, hopefully share a lot of laughter. Meals almost always end in dessert (which you'll see in Chapter 12 is traditionally very healthy), and the final course, coffee or espresso, which is savored slowly with more visiting.

Research has shown that eating slowly is good for you in many ways. First of all, it gives your body a chance to know if it's full before you throw an extra helping down your gullet. If it takes your body twenty minutes to feel full and you scarfed down dinner in ten, you're fighting a losing battle. Eating slowly and consciously, actually paying attention to what you're putting in your mouth (which I highly recommend in all instances), also helps you make better, healthier choices.

Delicious, healthy food demands to be savored. You want to share a gourmet, heart-healthy meal with your friends and family. Crappy, non-nutritious junk somehow begs to be eaten alone in our closet or smuggled in our purse or chomped down in the car.

Being in a constant state of hurry, worry, and stress is stressful for your health as well. It can stop you from sleeping well. It can cause you to choose closet-friendly junk food. It can rot your gut, mess with your brain chemicals, and actually slow your metabolism.

We all get into those periods when we're so busy, we don't realize we're taking care of everyone else but ourselves. I've heard lots of moms say that running around after kids and doing a ton of activities keeps them "moving" and eating less. But that kind of crazy, on-the-run lifestyle really isn't good for you. Moving around behind the wheel of a car chauffeuring your kids all day long is not exactly aerobic. And eating fewer healthy family meals but more things you find on the floor of your car is not a great long-term weight loss plan.

I've learned I have to make the time to take care of myself or I won't be any good to anyone. I still make quick meals, but I make sure everyone takes the time to sit down and enjoy them together (less time spent cooking means more time for eating!). For the first time in my life, I joined a gym. I hate exercising—which is probably why I've never done it before—but I'm finding out that I actually look forward to it because it's "me" time. The older girls are in school, I check Audriana into the child care, and I get to be alone to concentrate on my body, to build my strength and endurance, and sometimes for the only time all day, to actually read a magazine!

Working out also gives me two things I didn't know I was missing: endorphins and a sense of accomplishment. Everyone wants to feel like they're good at stuff, and I get enormous pleasure out of my work and my family, but after I work out, I'm proud of myself physically. I'm proud that I can take control of my own body, work off the extra wiggle, and tighten my muscles. Exercising also releases those feel-good hormones, endorphins, which not only give me a boost all day, but make me fall asleep faster and sleep more soundly.

So enjoy quick-cooking, but promise me you'll slow down whenever you aren't on the treadmill.

Treadmill Fun

I've never been a runner, and I just recently found out I like it. I'm naturally a fast walker, I move quickly through everything, but I never took time out to exercise. When I decided to start treating my body better, the first thing I did was run.

I just did my first 5K run with Joe and I loved the challenge of it. I am competitive and I liked the idea of pushing myself to see if I could do it and how fast. But living in Jersey, I can't always run outside. So I've become a treadmill girl.

I was nervous that it would get boring, but I've found that if you mix up your movements with every song you're listening to, it flies by and it's fun. First I walk to warm up, then I power walk, then I sprint, then I walk, then I skip, then I jog, then I sprint again, and so on. Sometimes I even bust out dance moves on the treadmill, and I throw my arms around to the music pretty much the whole time. Working out should be a celebration, not a chore. I'm thankful that I'm able to move my body, that I'm healthy and uninjured, and still young . . . well, young at heart anyway!

Italian Chicken Stir-Fry

Makes 4 servings

Joe makes this all the time—even when he's home alone—because it's so quick and easy. Once you've memorized this recipe, there's no excuse to ever dine alone on cereal or a frozen meal again! And it's great for guests and picky eaters since you can easily add or subtract ingredients. Plus it makes yummy leftovers.

2 tablespoons extra-virgin olive oil, divided

1 pound chicken tenderloins, cut into 3/4-inch chunks

1/2 teaspoon salt

1/4 teaspoon freshly ground black pepper

2 cups bite-sized broccoli florets

2 medium carrots, cut on the diagonal into 1/8-inch-thick slices

1 medium zucchini, halved lengthwise, and cut on the diagonal into 1/8-inch-thick slices

1 red bell pepper, cored, seeded, and cut into 1/4-inch-thick strips

1 teaspoon dried oregano

1 1/2 teaspoons cornstarch

1 cup reduced-sodium chicken broth

1. Heat 1 tablespoon of oil in a large skillet over medium-high heat. Season the chicken with the salt and pepper. Add to the skillet and cook, turning occasionally, until the chicken is nicely browned, about 4 minutes. Transfer to a plate.

2. Heat the remaining tablespoon oil in the skillet over medium-high heat. Add the broccoli, carrots, zucchini, and red pepper and cook, stirring often, until the vegetables begin to soften, about 3 minutes. Return the chicken to the skillet and add the oregano. Cook, stirring often, until the vegetables are crisp-tender and the chicken is cooked through, about 3 minutes.

3. Sprinkle the cornstarch over the broth in its measuring cup and stir to dissolve. Pour into the skillet and stir until the broth mixture comes to a boil and thickens. Serve hot.

Cavatappi Puttanesca

Makes 6 servings

In *Skinny Italian*, my puttanesca sauce was a reader favorite, I think just as much for the great taste as for the great story. *Puttanesca* literally means "prostitution whore sauce." It was invented by ladies of the evening who were only allowed a few minutes to grab items in the public market to make their dinner. There are as many variations as there are loose women in world (sadly). This time I'm giving you a version with peppers and tuna.

1 pound cavatappi pasta

1 tablespoon extra-virgin olive oil

1 red bell pepper, cored, seeded, and cut into ¼-inch dice

2 garlic cloves, minced

1 teaspoon anchovy paste (optional)

1 teaspoon dried oregano

¼ teaspoon red pepper flakes

1 (28-ounce) can Italian tomatoes in juice, chopped, with their juices

1 (6-ounce) can chunk white tuna in water, drained

½ cup pitted and coarsely chopped kalamata olives

3 tablespoons bottled capers, drained and rinsed

1. Bring a large pot of salted water to a boil over high heat. Add the cavatappi and cook according to the package directions until al dente.

2. Meanwhile, make the sauce. Heat the oil in a large saucepan over medium-high heat. Add the red bell pepper and cook, stirring often, until seared and beginning to soften, about 3 minutes. Reduce the heat to medium-low. Add the garlic, anchovy paste, if using, oregano, and red pepper flakes and stir almost constantly until the garlic is fragrant, about 30 seconds (the oil is hot and the garlic will cook quickly, so don't let it burn).

3. Add the tomatoes and their juices and return the heat to high. Add the tuna, olives, and capers and cook, stirring often and breaking up the tuna with a wooden spoon, until the tomato juices have slightly thickened, about 5 minutes. Remove from the heat and cover to keep warm.

4. When the pasta is cooked, drain in a colander. Return the pasta to its cooking pot. Add the sauce and mix well. Divide among 6 pasta bowls and serve hot.

Gnocchi with Pink Tomato Sauce

Makes 6 servings

It's taken me three books to finally get to gnocchi, but it was worth the wait! Gnocchi are little Italian dumplings made of cheese, flour, potato, or any combination of the three. Although they're filling and similarly colored, they aren't pasta! It is easy to make them from scratch, but since we're all about super-fast here, we're going to use premade gnocchi here. Look for vacuum-packed containers of potato and cheese gnocchi in the refrigerated section with the fresh pasta. And be warned, they cook very quickly; only a couple of minutes and you're done!

1 tablespoon extra-virgin olive oil

1 medium onion, finely chopped

2 garlic cloves, minced

1 (28-ounce) can Italian tomatoes in juice, chopped, with their juices

¼ cup tomato paste

2 tablespoons finely chopped fresh sage

¼ teaspoon red pepper flakes

1 cup low-fat ricotta cheese

2 (17.5-ounce) packages potato gnocchi

6 tablespoons freshly grated Parmigiano-Reggiano or Parmesan cheese, for serving

1. Bring a large pot of salted water to a boil over high heat.

2. Meanwhile, heat the oil in a large saucepan over medium heat. Add the onion and cook, stirring often, until softened, about 3 minutes. Stir in the garlic and cook, stirring often, until fragrant, about 1 minute. Stir in the tomatoes with their juices, the tomato paste, sage, and red pepper flakes. Bring to a boil over high heat. Reduce the heat to medium-low and let simmer for 10 minutes. Remove from the heat, add the ricotta, and whisk until smooth. Cover to keep warm.

3. Add the gnocchi to the boiling water and cook according to the package directions until they float on the surface of the water. Drain in a colander. Return the gnocchi to their cooking pot. Add the sauce and stir well. Divide among 6 pasta bowls. Sprinkle each with 1 tablespoon of Parmesan cheese and serve hot.

Ligurian Burrida (Seafood Stew)

Makes 6 servings

Popular in Liguria, the coastal region of northwest Italy, the word *burrida* comes from the French Provençal dialect word, *bourrido*, which means "to boil." That should give you some idea how to cook it. Once the onions and garlic have cooked, boil the hell out of the rest of the ingredients so the stew cooks fast.

1 tablespoon extra-virgin olive oil

1 medium onion, chopped

3 garlic cloves, minced

1 (28-ounce) can Italian tomatoes in juice, chopped, juices reserved

1 (8-ounce) bottle clam juice

2 tablespoons chopped fresh Italian parsley

¼ teaspoon red pepper flakes

1 pound littleneck clams, scrubbed and rinsed

1 pound skinless halibut or cod fillets, cut into 1-inch pieces

½ pound large (21/25 count) shrimp, peeled and deveined

1. Heat the oil in a large saucepan over medium heat. Add the onion and cook, stirring occasionally, until softened, about 3 minutes. Stir in the garlic and cook, stirring often, until fragrant, about 1 minute. Add the tomatoes with their juices, the clam juice, 1 cup water, and the parsley and red pepper flakes. Bring to a boil over high heat. Cook, stirring often, until the tomato juices are slightly thickened, about 5 minutes.

2. Add the clams and cover. Cook, shaking the saucepan occasionally, until the clams are just beginning to open, about 3 minutes. Move the clams over in the pot to make some room, and add the cod and shrimp, submerging them in the cooking liquid. Cover again and cook until the fish is opaque and all of the clams are open, about 5 minutes. Discard any clams that do not open. Divide the seafood and broth among 6 soup bowls and serve hot.

Cappellini with Two-Tomato Sauce and Basil

Makes 6 servings

Thin pasta needs a light sauce—heavy meat sauces are a bad match for the delicate strands of cappellini, spaghettini, or angel hair. While this tomato sauce isn't hefty, it is full of flavor from two kinds of tomatoes and a lot of fresh basil. It is a good base for adding your own favorites—sautéed mushrooms, cooked seafood, and artichoke hearts are a few ideas—but you will probably love it just the way it is.

1 tablespoon extra-virgin olive oil

2 garlic cloves, minced

1 (14.5-ounce) can Italian tomatoes in juice, chopped, with their juices

1 pint grape tomatoes, halved lengthwise

½ cup (packed) coarsely chopped fresh basil, plus more for serving

¼ teaspoon red pepper flakes

1 pound whole-wheat cappellini, thin spaghetti, or angel hair pasta

6 tablespoons freshly grated Parmigiano-Reggiano or Parmesan cheese, for serving

1. Bring a large pot of lightly salted water to a boil over high heat.

2. Meanwhile, make the sauce. Heat the oil and garlic together in a large saucepan over medium-low heat, stirring often, until the garlic has softened, about 2 minutes. Add the canned tomatoes and their juices, the grape tomatoes, basil, and red pepper flakes. Bring to a boil over high heat. Reduce the heat to medium and cook, stirring often, until the tomato juices are slightly thickened, about 5 minutes. Remove from the heat and cover to keep warm.

3. Add the pasta to the boiling water and cook according to the package directions until al dente. Scoop out and reserve ½ cup of the pasta cooking water. Drain the pasta in a colander. Return the pasta to its cooking pot. Add the sauce and reserved cooking water and stir well. Divide among 6 pasta bowls. Sprinkle each with 1 tablespoon of Parmesan cheese and more chopped fresh basil and serve hot.

Penne Primavera

Makes 6 servings

Named for the Italian word for "spring," this light and easy pasta dish celebrates the best flavors of the season. Luckily, we can get them all year round! The shallots give the sauce a nice bite, and anything with peas is a favorite in my house.

1 pound whole-wheat penne
   or ziti pasta

1 tablespoon extra-virgin olive oil

1 medium zucchini, cut into thin
   half-moons

3 tablespoons finely chopped
   shallots

1 pint grape tomatoes,
   halved lengthwise

1 cup frozen thawed peas

2 tablespoons finely chopped fresh
   basil, oregano, or Italian parsley

½ teaspoon salt

¼ teaspoon freshly ground
   black pepper

½ cup low-fat ricotta cheese

6 tablespoons freshly grated
   Romano or Parmesan cheese

1. Bring a large pot of lightly salted water to a boil over high heat. Add the penne and cook according to the package directions until al dente.

2. Meanwhile, make the sauce. Heat the oil in a large saucepan over medium-high heat. Add the zucchini and cook, stirring occasionally, until softened, about 5 minutes. Stir in the shallots and cook, stirring occasionally, until softened, about 1 minute. Add the grape tomatoes, peas, and basil and cook, stirring often, until the tomatoes give off their juices and collapse, about 5 minutes. Remove from the heat and cover to keep warm. Season with the salt and pepper.

3. When the pasta is cooked, scoop out and reserve 1 cup of the pasta cooking water. Drain the pasta in a colander. Return the pasta to its cooking pot. Add the vegetable mixture and ricotta cheese. Stir, adding enough of the reserved pasta water to make a creamy sauce. Divide among 6 pasta bowls. Sprinkle each with 1 tablespoon of the Romano cheese and serve hot.

Salmon alla Sala Consilina

Makes 4 servings

While Sala Consilina, the town where my parents are from and where I was conceived, is inland in Italy, it's still less than twenty miles from the Tyrrhenian Sea. Seafood is a huge part of the healthy cuisine. We eat lots of fish—tilapia, sole, salmon, cod, even baccalà. Here's one of my favorite ways to prepare it.

4 (6-ounce) skinless center-cut salmon fillets

2 tablespoons extra-virgin olive oil, divided

1/2 teaspoon salt

1/4 teaspoon freshly ground black pepper

1 (14.5-ounce) can petite diced tomatoes, drained

1/4 cup dry white wine, such as Pinot Grigio

1/4 cup finely chopped fresh basil leaves

2 tablespoons freshly squeezed lemon juice

1 teaspoon finely chopped fresh thyme

1. Preheat the oven to 400ºF. Have ready four 12-inch-square pieces of alumninum foil (nonstick foil works great for this recipe).

2. Brush the salmon on both sides with 1 tablespoon of oil and season with the salt and pepper. Combine the drained tomatoes, wine, basil, lemon juice, remaining 1 tablespoon oil, and thyme in a medium bowl.

3. For each serving, place a salmon fillet in the center of a foil square. Spoon one-quarter of the tomato mixture, with its juices, over the salmon, slightly curving up the 4 sides of the foil, if needed, to contain the juices. Fold the foil into a packet, tightly closing the long seam on top and the 2 sides. Transfer to a rimmed baking sheet.

4. Bake until the salmon is barely opaque in the center (open a packet to check), about 20 minutes. Serve hot.

Gemelli L'Estate

Makes 6 servings

I decided to follow the spring pasta with a dish named for summer. *L'estate* [leh-STAH-tay] is my favorite time of year. Yes, this includes a lot of spring vegetables, but to me the star of this dish is the sun-drenched flavor of the sun-dried tomatoes. Is there anything more fabulous than sunshine? Maybe sunshine on the beach after eating Gemelli L'Estate . . .

1 pound gemelli or short fusilli pasta

1 tablespoon extra-virgin olive oil

2 garlic cloves, minced

1 (8-ounce) bag frozen thawed artichoke hearts, coarsely chopped

½ cup drained and coarsely chopped sun-dried tomatoes in oil

½ cup pitted and coarsely chopped kalamata olives

½ cup reduced-sodium chicken broth

3 tablespoons finely chopped fresh basil, oregano, or Italian parsley, plus more for serving

2 tablespoons freshly squeezed lemon juice

¼ teaspoon red pepper flakes

6 tablespoons freshly grated Parmigiano-Reggiano or Parmesan cheese, for serving

1. Bring a large pot of salted water to a boil over high heat. Add the gemelli and cook according to the package directions until al dente.

2. Meanwhile, make the sauce. Heat the oil and garlic together in a large saucepan over medium-low heat, stirring often, until the garlic is softened, about 2 minutes. Add the artichoke hearts, sun-dried tomatoes, olives, broth, basil, lemon juice, and red pepper flakes and bring to a simmer. Cover and cook, stirring often, until the artichokes are heated through, about 2 minutes. Remove from the heat and cover to keep warm.

3. When the gemelli is cooked, drain in a colander. Return the gemelli to its cooking pot. Add the artichoke mixture and the Parmesan, and stir well. Divide among 6 pasta bowls. Sprinkle each with chopped basil, and serve hot.

CHAPTER 10

Spice It Up—
Some Like It HOT

I think you know by now I like things hot. I love summer, I have a hot Italian temper, and I love, love, love hot and spicy food.

Spicy food isn't just fun to eat (and fun to watch people who can't handle it eat); it's also really good for you. My first thought as to *why* was that people probably eat smaller portions of fiery foods. But when I looked into it, I found that the capsaicin that gives hot peppers their kick is really a feisty little thing. The American Association for Cancer Research believes capsaicin can slow the growth of cancer cells, especially in the pancreas, and can actually cause cancer cells to die. The American Chemistry Society published a study that showed evidence that capsaicin helps fight fat buildup and can cause weight loss. And according to *USA Today*, hot peppers help heart health, can reduce cholesterol, help people with asthma and respiratory illnesses breathe better, and even help you feel better when you have a cold or the flu.

Eating spicy food can also cause your body's metabolism to speed up, and your brain to release those delicious endorphins, to help you push through the burning sensation on your tongue.

Using hot seasonings in your cooking can be a great way to cut down on your salt consumption, since you won't need any extra "bite."

If you're new to spicy food, or don't tolerate it very well, you can get your body used to it. It's not actually "hot" food. What you feel in your mouth is a little irritation that over time your body will get used to. Start with cooler peppers—like pimentos and pepperoncini—and work your way up. If you are using hot fresh chiles, such as jalapeños, always cut out the ribs and seeds. Keep the seeds because if a sauce is too mild, you can add them to increase the spiciness.

Don't overdo it, of course. And if you need quick relief, grab a glass of milk. The casein in milk will help wash the capsaicin out of your mouth.

FABULICIOUS FITNESS:
Hot Workouts

I am learning to love working out, and I love heat, but I'm not ready to do that Hot Yoga sweat lodge stuff. But to keep from getting bored, you should definitely spice up your workout routine. Don't just do one thing or your body will get used to it. If you favor the treadmill, trade it for the bike or the elliptical some days.

I think the biggest problem most people have with working out is keeping at it. It's so easy to get bored or too busy. One of my secrets to staying interested is to spice up my outfits. Who wants to look like a frumpy mess at the gym? Go get a hot work-out outfit. They even have shapers that will help suck you in just a little so you can strut your stuff more confidently, even as you're working toward a better body. Don't hide yourself in black. Get the bright spandex and shine! You are doing amazing things for your body, and you should be proud of yourself!

Linguine Indiavolati

Makes 6 servings

In Italian, *indiavolati* means "furious." I love that. Only the Italians would decide to make a furious pasta! The crushed hot red pepper flakes mixed with cayenne pepper give this a crazy kick, and the bay scallops provide lots of protein, vitamin B-12, omega-3, and tryptophan. The only thing that would make me mad about this pasta is if Joe didn't save me some!

1 tablespoon extra-virgin olive oil

3 garlic cloves, minced

1 (28-ounce) can Italian tomatoes in juice, chopped, with their juices

½ teaspoon salt

½ teaspoon red pepper flakes

¼ teaspoon cayenne pepper

3 cups bite-sized broccoli florets

1 pound whole-wheat linguine pasta

½ pound bay scallops

2 tablespoons finely chopped fresh Italian parsley, basil, or oregano

1. Bring a large pot of salted water to a boil over high heat.

2. Meanwhile, start the sauce. Heat the oil and garlic together in a large saucepan over medium-low heat, stirring often, until the garlic has softened, about 2 minutes. Add the tomatoes with their juices, salt, red pepper flakes, and cayenne pepper and bring to a boil over high heat. Reduce the heat to medium-low and simmer, stirring often, until the tomato juices are slightly thickened, about 10 minutes. Remove from the heat.

3. Add the broccoli to the boiling water and cook until crisp-tender, about 4 minutes. Using a wire sieve, scoop out the broccoli from the water and transfer to a bowl. Add the linguine to the water and cook according to the package directions until al dente.

4. About 5 minutes before the linguine is done, return the sauce to medium-high heat and bring to a boil. Stir in the scallops, broccoli, and parsley and cook, stirring occasionally, until the scallops are opaque, about 4 minutes.

5. Drain the linguine in a colander. Return the linguine to its pot. Add the scallop mixture and mix well. Divide among 6 pasta bowls and serve hot.

When in Rome . . .

Indiavolati = in-dee-AH-vo-lah-tee

Shrimp Salad with Diablo Dressing

Makes 4 servings

I love the cool crunch of the lettuce topped with the spicy "devil" dressing. This quick and easy salad is the perfect pick-me-up after a hard day's work (or workout!). It's got just the right balance of fiber and protein, and it's so pretty and colorful, I can't help but smile when I eat it. You can also use the dressing as a marinade, a sandwich spread, or brushed over grilled shrimp.

2 garlic cloves, crushed under the flat side of a chef's knife and peeled

½ teaspoon salt

2 tablespoons red wine vinegar

2 tablespoons extra-virgin olive oil

1 tablespoon freshly squeezed lemon juice

½ teaspoon dried oregano

½ teaspoon red pepper flakes

1 (5-ounce) container mixed salad greens

2 ripe plum (Roma) tomatoes, cut into ½-inch chunks

1 pound chilled cooked, peeled, and deveined shrimp

1. To make the dressing, chop the garlic cloves on a cutting board. Sprinkle with the salt, and chop, mince, and smear the garlic on the board to make a rough paste. Transfer to a jar. Add 3 tablespoons water, the vinegar, oil, lemon juice, oregano, and red pepper flakes to the jar. Secure the lid on the jar and shake well to combine.

2. Spread the salad greens on a serving platter and add the tomatoes. Mix the shrimp with the dressing. Using a slotted spoon, heap the shrimp on top of the salad, and drizzle the dressing over all. Serve immediately.

Hot Mussels Marinara

Makes 6 servings

This is my dad's famous appetizer, maybe the hottest version on the planet. The way we make it, it's so hot most people who visit our house can't go near it. But me and my dad, and my husband, Joe, we can't get enough of it. I'm gonna start you off easy though, with just 1/4 teaspoon of cayenne.

2 pounds mussels, scrubbed

1 tablespoon extra-virgin olive oil

1 (14.5-ounce) can diced petite tomatoes, with their juices

2 tablespoons tomato paste

2 tablespoons finely chopped fresh basil

1/4 teaspoon cayenne pepper, or more to taste

2 tablespoons finely chopped fresh Italian parsley

Note: I won't tell you what my father calls the little beards on mussels, but it's very important you remove them. If you don't know how, get your fish guy to do it for you.

1. Preheat the oven to 400ºF.

2. If the mussels have beards (hairy knots connected to the shells), pull the beards off with pliers. Place the mussels in a large saucepan and add 1/2 cup water. Cover and cook over high heat, occasionally shaking the pan, until the mussels open, about 6 minutes. Discard any mussels that do not open.

3. Meanwhile, make a sauce. Heat the oil in a large saucepan over medium heat. Add the tomatoes and their juices, the tomato paste, 1/4 cup water, the basil, and cayenne pepper. Bring to a boil and cook, stirring often, until the sauce has thickened, about 10 minutes. Remove from the heat. Season with more cayenne pepper, if you wish.

3. Pour the mussels into a bowl and let cool until easy to handle. Remove the top shell half from each mussel, keeping the mussel meat in the bottom half. Arrange the shells, with the mussels facing up, on a rimmed baking sheet. Fill each shell with a generous teaspoon of the sauce. (If desired, cool the mussel juice left in the pan, cover, and freeze for up to 1 month. It is a good substitute for bottled clam juice.)

4. Bake until the tomato sauce looks somewhat drier, about 10 minutes. Transfer to a serving platter, sprinkle with parsley, and serve hot.

Spicy Pork Choplets

Makes 4 servings

One of my favorite things about this recipe isn't the spice, it's the sage. The sweet, savory herb goes so well with the juicy pork and chili powder. And as far as helping your brain, sage is no joke. Sage has been used for over a thousand years to treat neurological diseases, and modern research shows that sage does boost memory and can even help fight Alzheimer's.

2 tablespoons extra-virgin olive oil, divided

4 (6-ounce) boneless pork chops, each about ½-inch thick

½ teaspoon salt

4 garlic cloves, thinly sliced

1 (15-ounce) can Italian tomatoes in juice, chopped, with their juices

¼ cup dry white wine, such as Pinot Grigio

2 tablespoons finely chopped fresh sage

1 teaspoon chili powder

¼ teaspoon red pepper flakes

1. Heat 1 tablespoon of oil in a large skillet over medium-high heat. Season the pork chops with the salt. Add to the skillet and cook until the undersides are lightly browned, about 2 minutes. Flip the chops and brown the other sides, about 2 minutes more. Transfer to a plate.

2. Add the remaining 1 tablespoon oil and the garlic to the same skillet. Stir over medium heat until the garlic is golden, about 30 minutes. (The skillet will be hot and the garlic will cook quickly, so don't let it burn.) Add the tomatoes, wine, sage, chili powder, and red pepper flakes. Bring to a boil. Reduce the heat to medium-low and simmer for 5 minutes.

3. Return the pork chops and any juices from the plate to the skillet. Simmer until the pork shows no sign of pink when pierced in the center with a knife, about 7 minutes. Serve hot.

Spaghettini alla Carrettiera

Makes 6 servings

This is another dish that comes from the rustic Italian workers' need to eat on the job. *Carrettieri* were donkey-cart drivers who brought goods from the countryside into the cities and marketplaces. They improvised their meals with whatever they could find—usually mushrooms and wild herbs—and made it quickly so they could get back on the road. It's simple, speedy, and super-satisfying!

2 tablespoons extra-virgin olive oil

10 ounces thinly sliced cremini (baby bella) mushrooms

4 garlic cloves, minced

1 (28-ounce) can Italian tomatoes in juice, chopped, with their juices

2 tablespoons finely chopped fresh Italian parsley, basil, or oregano, plus more for serving

¼ teaspoon red pepper flakes

1 pound whole-wheat cappellini, thin spaghetti, or angel hair pasta

6 tablespoons freshly grated Romano cheese, for serving

1. Bring a large pot of salted water to a boil over high heat.

2. Heat the oil in a large saucepan over medium-high heat. Add the mushrooms and cook, stirring occasionally, until they are sizzling in their own juices, about 6 minutes. Add the garlic and stir until it is fragrant, about 1 minute. Stir in the tomatoes with their juices, the parsley, and red pepper flakes and bring to a boil. Cook, stirring occasionally, until the juices have slightly thickened, about 5 minutes. Remove from the heat and cover to keep warm.

3. About 5 minutes before the sauce is done, add the cappellini to the boiling water and cook until al dente according to the package directions. Drain the cappellini and return the pasta to its cooking pot. Add the tomato sauce and mix well. Divide among 6 pasta bowls. Sprinkle each with 1 tablespoon of cheese and some chopped fresh parsley, and serve hot.

CHAPTER 11

Sex It Up—
Romantic Meals

I don't have to tell you that sex is a good workout (well, if you're doing it right). Any aerobic activity, especially one that releases all kinds of happy hormones, is going to benefit your health. But to be healthier longer than just those 15 (5? 3?) minutes, you can add one very important thing: love.

It's always seemed to me that being in a relationship is good for your health. How else do you explain the people who've been married for 60 years and die within months—or even minutes!—of each other? I think your loved ones keep you going. And apparently, I'm not alone. There are tons of reports about how being surrounded by love can reduce your blood pressure, help fight depression, and even help you live longer. Researchers at Brigham Young University studied more than 300,000 people and found that the people with a solid circle of family, friends, and neighbors can "increase their survival rate" by 50 percent. They compared the bad effects of being lonely and isolating yourself with smoking 15 cigarettes a day or being an alcoholic! How crazy is that?

Your health supposedly gets even better if you get married. The U.S. Department of Health and Human Services released a huge report in 2007 that said married men and women were not only healthier, but they also lived much longer than unmarried people. Unmarried people supposedly also spend twice as long in the hospital as married people. And they even say you have a greater chance of beating cancer if you're married.

I think the most obvious reason is the fact that people who are married (for

Motivating Music

The best way to power through a workout is with high-intensity music that just begs you to move your body. Here's the playlist that gets my blood flowing:

- "I Gotta Feeling" Black Eyed Peas
- "Give Me Everything" Pitbull
- "I Wanna Go" Britney Spears
- "The Fame" Lady Gaga
- "Down" Jay Sean
- "Break Your Heart" Taio Cruz
- "I Like It" Enrique Iglesias
- "Right Round" Flo Rida
- "Let it Rock" Kevin Rudolf
- "Disturbia" Rihanna
- "On the Floor" Jennifer Lopez
- "Sexy and I Know It" LMFAO

better or for worse!) are physically there for each other (for better or for worse!). Being in a couple means you have someone to help protect you from the outside world, someone to build you up, to support you through hard times, and to encourage you to take better care of yourself. And you do the same for them!

I'm an old-fashioned girl who went from her parents' house to her husband's. I've been married for twelve years now. It's not always a picnic of course—although

Joe did surprise me on our last anniversary with an actual picnic in our dining room—but it's incredibly rewarding. I don't know what I'd do without my support system, not just my husband and my kids, but my family and my amazing friends.

Your loved ones are great resources for keeping you on a healthy path. Get your whole family to eat healthier together. Get a workout buddy to keep you motivated. Next time you feel like drowning your sorrows in a bag of Doritos®, call a friend first. And be there for your inner circle as well. Don't look the other way when your friend falls off the wagon or your hubby tries to order a hamburger bigger than his bicep. Support is a huge part of success.

Like any fire, to keep your relationships going, you have to feed them. Taking something for granted is the easiest way to lose it. As busy as life gets, you have to make time for your loved ones. And there's no easier way to do that than over a beautiful meal. You have to eat anyway; you might as well use the opportunity to hang out with the ones you love.

In Italian families, Sunday dinner is a huge part of keeping a family together. And for Joe and me, we make Friday night "date" night. Every single Friday night. It's not always easy to carve out that time for ourselves, especially since we have four young daughters, and sometimes we don't even go anywhere. We've spent many date nights alone on the couch after the kids have gone to bed. But it's something we do for ourselves and our relationship, to keep things strong, to remind each other of why we love the other person, and to hopefully get around to some late-night calorie burning.

More than any other request, I get people writing me asking for romantic dinner ideas. Here's a whole chapter of them. Delicious, healthy dishes to help you keep the heat turned up at home.

Sexy Chickpea Chard Stew

Makes 4 servings

I know what you're thinking: "Sexy" does not belong next to the words "chickpea" and "chard." Once you eat this though, you'll change your mind! Chickpeas (also called garbanzo beans) are great to add to any healthy diet because they are so so good for you, but their buttery texture makes you feel like you're eating something sinful. And many people believe chickpeas are a powerful aphrodisiac, especially for men. You can make this for your man, and get back to me.

1 tablespoon extra-virgin olive oil

1 cup thinly sliced shallots

2 garlic cloves, minced

2 pounds Swiss chard, trimmed, well rinsed, but not dried

1 (15-ounce) can chickpeas (garbanzo beans), drained and rinsed

3 ripe plum (Roma) tomatoes, seeded and cut into 1/2-inch dice

1 cup canned vegetable broth or reduced-sodium chicken broth

3/4 teaspoon salt

1/4 teaspoon cayenne pepper

Lemon wedges, for serving

1. Heat the oil in a large saucepan over medium heat. Add the shallots and cook, stirring occasionally, until softened, about 2 minutes. Stir in the garlic and cook until fragrant, about 1 minute.

2. Meanwhile, cut off the stems from the chard. Cut the stems crosswise into 1/4-inch-thick slices. Coarsely chop the chard leaves.

3. In batches, add the chard leaves and stems with any clinging water to the saucepan, letting the first batch wilt before adding more. Stir in the chickpeas, tomatoes, broth, salt, and cayenne pepper and bring to a boil. Reduce the heat to medium-low and cover. Simmer, stirring occasionally, until the stems are just tender, about 12 minutes.

4. Divide the stew among 6 soup bowls, add the lemon wedges to squeeze over each portion, and serve hot.

Chicken di Firenze

Makes 4 servings

Whenever you see an Italian dish named for Florence, you can expect lots of delicious spinach. This chicken is no exception. We've already established that spinach is one of the world's best vegetables in terms of nutrient density. This recipe establishes its taste dominance as well. It's the kind of dish that you'd find in an upscale Italian restaurant yet can be made at home with no problem. It's almost impossible not to feel romantic eating the juicy chicken on a bed of tender spinach mixed with creamy low-fat ricotta.

....

1 tablespoon extra-virgin olive oil, plus more for the baking dish

1/2 cup chopped shallots

2 garlic cloves, minced

2 pounds fresh leaf spinach, tough stems removed, well rinsed but not dried, coarsely chopped

1/3 cup drained coarsely chopped sun-dried tomatoes in oil

3/4 teaspoon salt, divided

1/4 teaspoon red pepper flakes

1/2 cup low-fat ricotta cheese

1 pound chicken tenderloins

1/4 teaspoon freshly ground black pepper

1. Preheat the oven to 350ºF. Lightly oil a 13 x 9-inch baking dish.

2. Heat the oil in a large saucepan over medium heat. Add the shallots and garlic and cook until the shallots are softened, about 2 minutes. In batches, stir in the spinach with any clinging water, letting the first batch wilt before adding more. Stir in the sun-dried tomatoes, 1/4 teaspoon of salt, and the red pepper flakes. Cook until the spinach is tender, about 3 minutes. Drain well in a colander. Press the spinach mixture with a rubber spatula to remove excess moisture, but don't make the spinach too dry. Transfer to a bowl and stir in the ricotta cheese. Spread in the prepared baking dish.

3. Season the chicken tenderloins with the remaining 1/2 teaspoon salt and the pepper. Submerge the tenderloins in the spinach mixture, leaving the tops of the tenderloins exposed. Bake until the chicken shows no sign of pink when pierced in the center with a sharp knife, about 15 minutes. Serve hot.

Heavenly Halibut

Makes 4 servings

You know fish is good for your body, but it's also good for your sex life. MSNBC reported that the nutrients in halibut, especially, can enhance your libido because they help regulate testosterone levels and healthy blood circulation (I'll let you figure that last one out). This quick, light, and delicious meal is the perfect prelude to a romantic night in.

Extra-virgin olive oil, for the
   baking dish
4 skinless halibut fillets
   (about 6 ounces each)
1/2 teaspoon salt
1/4 teaspoon freshly ground
   black pepper
1/4 cup dry white wine
1/4 cup reduced-sodium
   chicken broth
2 tablespoons freshly squeezed
   lemon juice
1 tablespoon finely chopped chives
1 tablespoon finely chopped fresh
   Italian parsley
1 tablespoon finely chopped
   fresh tarragon

1. Preheat the oven to 450ºF. Lightly oil a 13 x 9-inch baking dish.

2. Season the halibut with the salt and pepper. Place the halibut in the baking dish. Mix the wine, broth, lemon juice, chives, parsley, and tarragon in a small bowl. Spoon the mixture over the halibut.

3. Bake until the halibut is opaque when pierced in the center with the tip of a sharp knife, about 15 minutes. Transfer each fillet to a dinner plate, top each with equal amounts of the cooking liquid, and serve hot.

Italian Flank Steak with Smothered Onions

Makes 6 servings

My mama makes the best flank steak in the world. We all look forward to it not just for dinner, but for the delicious leftovers for days afterward; this is great cut up on salads especially. A juicy steak is definitely the way to a man's heart, as my father and my husband love, love, love this recipe! I learned from the best, but I do add an extra step my mom doesn't: I sear the steak first for some extra flavor and color. My mom does the whole thing in the oven. I don't mind if you want to make it both ways—it comes out amazing no matter what!

2 tablespoons extra-virgin
   olive oil, divided

1 flank steak (about 1¾ pounds)

1 teaspoon salt, divided

½ teaspoon freshly ground
   black pepper, divided

8 large onions, cut into
   ¼-inch-thick half-moons

½ cup reduced-sodium beef broth

½ cup hearty red wine,
   such as Shiraz

1 tablespoon finely chopped
   fresh Italian parsley

Note: Garlic and onions are delicious, and as long as you and your loved one are eating the same thing, you won't have a problem with non-sexy breath.

1. Preheat the oven to 400°F.

2. Heat 1 tablespoon of oil in a very large skillet over medium-high heat. Season the steak with ½ teaspoon salt and ¼ teaspoon pepper. Add to the skillet and cook until the underside is browned, about 2 minutes. Flip the steak and brown the other side, about 2 minutes more. Transfer to a large roasting pan.

3. Heat the remaining tablespoon of oil in the skillet. Add the onions (they will be crowded) and cover. Cook, stirring occasionally, until the onions are wilted, about 10 minutes. Add the broth and wine and bring to a boil. Cook the onions, uncovered, stirring occasionally, until the liquid is slightly reduced, about 5 minutes. Season with the remaining ½ teaspoon salt and ¼ teaspoon pepper. Spread over the steak in the roasting pan.

4. Bake until the onions are very tender and an instant-read thermometer inserted horizontally into the side of the steak reads 130°F for medium, about 35 minutes. Transfer the steak to a cutting board (leave the onions in the oven) and let stand 5 minutes.

5. Using a sharp, thin knife held at a 45-degree angle, cut the steak across the grain into thin slices. Transfer to a platter. Spoon the onions around the steak, sprinkle with the parsley, and serve hot.

Red Snapper with Herbed Tomato Sauce

Makes 4 servings

I'm all about equal opportunity in the kitchen, and this is one of the things Joe loves to make for me. There's nothing more romantic than being part of a team, of a give-and-take partnership. Whether you make this for your loved one, or let them make it for you, it's a fantastic fish because it soaks up the flavors you add (in this case, a fresh, peppery, basil-tomato taste).

2 tablespoons extra-virgin olive oil

1 medium onion, chopped

2 garlic cloves, minced

1 (28-ounce) can diced tomatoes, undrained

2 tablespoons finely chopped fresh basil, plus more for serving

4 skinless red snapper fillets (about 6 ounces each)

½ teaspoon salt

¼ teaspoon freshly ground black pepper

1. Heat the oil in a large skillet over medium heat. Add the onion and cook, stirring occasionally, until softened, about 3 minutes. Stir in the garlic and cook until fragrant, about 1 minute more. Add the tomatoes with their juices and the 2 tablespoons basil. Bring to a boil. Cook at a brisk simmer, stirring occasionally, until the tomato juices are slightly thickened, about 5 minutes.

2. Season the snapper fillets with the salt and pepper. Nestle the fillets in the sauce and cover. Reduce the heat to medium-low. Simmer until the fillets are opaque when pierced in the center with the tip of a sharp knife, about 12 minutes.

3. Using a slotted metal spatula, transfer each fillet to a dinner plate and top each with equal amounts of the sauce. Sprinkle with additional basil and serve hot.

Pesce all' Acqua Pazza

Makes 4 servings

This is my absolute favorite recipe name. It means "fish in crazy water." It comes from Napoli fishermen who used to cook the catch of the day in seawater. The dish can take many forms, and there are recipes that have everything but the kitchen sink in the water. This one is only kinda crazy, but really, really good. Use any kind of fish you like, but it is best with something firm and meaty like Chilean sea bass or halibut. Adjust the cooking time accordingly for the thickness of the fillets.

1 tablespoon extra-virgin olive oil

½ cup chopped red onion

2 garlic cloves, minced

1 pint grape tomatoes, halved lengthwise

½ cup dry white wine

1 lemon, sliced into thin rounds

4 skinless Chilean sea bass fillets (about 6 ounces each)

¼ teaspoon salt

⅛ teaspoon freshly ground black pepper

3 tablespoons chopped fresh Italian parsley, for serving

1. Heat the oil in a large skillet over medium heat. Add the onion and cook, stirring often, until softened, about 3 minutes. Stir in the garlic and cook until it is fragrant, about 1 minute. Add 2 cups water, the tomatoes, wine, and lemon slices and bring to a boil. Reduce the heat to medium-low and simmer to blend the flavors without reducing for 10 minutes.

2. Place the fish in the simmering liquid and cover. Simmer until the fish is opaque when pierced in the center, about 15 minutes. Using a slotted spatula, transfer each fillet and one-quarter of the solids to each of 4 soup bowls. Tent each bowl with aluminum foil to keep warm.

3. Increase the heat under the skillet to high. Boil, stirring often, until the cooking liquid is reduced by half, about 5 minutes. Season with the salt and pepper. Uncover the bowls and discard the foil. Divide the reduced cooking liquid equally among the bowls and sprinkle each with the parsley. Serve hot.

CHAPTER 12

Sweeten It Up—
Guilt-Free Desserts

I'm all about dessert. I've got a huge sweet tooth. But I want to know when I'm indulging and when I'm being tricked into thinking a sweet isn't quite that bad for you. Nothing makes me madder than finding out I ate a dessert that had a million hidden calories and that frankly, wasn't even worth it. Sometimes the worst offenders don't even look that unhealthy!

In general, no matter what kind of nuts they put on the top, muffins, especially store-bought ones, are about the worst thing you can eat. Followed by most moist cakes, brownies, and ice cream with a vending machine's supply of candy chopped into it.

On the flip side, some things that just look so fattening, like creamy puddings, aren't always that bad. So how can you tell? First, get to know the good ingredients from the bad. Here's a quick list of the things that generally spell diet disaster in a dessert:

7 DEADLY SINNERS

- VEGETABLE OIL
- HEAVY CREAM
- MILK CHOCOLATE
- SHORTENING
- CARAMEL/BUTTERSCOTCH
- CREAM CHEESE
- PEANUT BUTTER

You can still enjoy some of the things in the list above, as long as they are just small parts of the dessert, something you lightly sprinkle on top. A couple curls of milk chocolate on fresh fruit? Go for it. Peanut butter-filled cookie? Take a pass.

Like everything, it's all about moderation. You can eat a bucketful of light popcorn and still pack on the pounds. A tiny square of the world's richest chocolate every now and then isn't likely to throw your metabolism out of whack.

When looking through my favorite Italian desserts for this book, I was happy to find that most of them were naturally low-fat and low-calorie. In Italy, we eat a lot of fruit and nuts; even our famous Italian cookies are relatively healthy compared to their American cousins.

Of course, there were one or two that I wanted to try to make healthier without completely turning them into bland diet food, specifically my mother-in-law's tiramisù. But like I promised in the beginning, I'm not going to reach for a "diet" food I would never use: no agave nectar or stewed prunes. You can make pretty amazing desserts just by making a few simple swaps—low-fat ricotta cheese for full fat. If you need a chemistry degree to figure out how to make a million substitutions, it's probably not a dessert worth making in the first place.

None of the desserts here use any of the 7 Deadly Sinners. They're all low-calorie and low-fat, and they are all insanely delicious.

Espresso Granita

Makes 6 servings

I ate this all the time when I was a kid (explains a lot, right?), but not because my mother gave it to me. She would make it as a frosty treat for herself, and I would sneak it out of the freezer. This is super-easy to make, you just want to stop by the freezer every half hour or so to give it a good mix so it will have that fabulous grainy texture. Serve with a dollop of fat-free whipped cream on top, or drizzle a spoonful of nonfat half-and-half over it.

3 ½ cups hot brewed Italian or
   French roast coffee
²/₃ cup (packed) light brown sugar

1. Place a 13 x 9-inch metal baking dish and a large metal spoon in the freezer to chill.

2. Stir the hot coffee and brown sugar together in a heatproof bowl to dissolve the sugar. Let cool completely.

3. Pour the coffee mixture into the chilled baking dish. Freeze until the mixture is icy around the edges, about 1 hour, depending on the freezer's temperature. Using the metal spoon, mix the frozen edges into the center (leave the spoon in the pan). Continue to freeze, repeating the stirring procedure about every 30 minutes, until the mixture has a slushy consistency, about 3 hours total freezing time.

4. Divide the granita equally among 6 chilled dessert bowls. Serve immediately.

Mixed Berry Zabaglione

Makes 6 servings

I know it's shocking that something that seems so decadent has a little more than 100 calories and 3 grams of fat per serving, but zabaglione cream is shockingly good. As with all things, you should practice moderation, but drizzled over fresh berries, it's a great way to get not only fiber and antioxidants from the fruit, but protein from the eggs as well. The secret to the low calorie count? No butter, no oil, no chocolate, no cheese. Just eggs, a little sugar, and a splash of wine. And love. Lots of love.

3 (6-ounce) containers fresh berries, such as raspberries, blueberries, and blackberries

4 large egg yolks plus 1 large egg white

⅓ cup sweet Marsala wine

3 tablespoons granulated sugar

½ teaspoon vanilla extract

1. Divide the berries equally among 6 large wine glasses. Set aside at room temperature.

2. Bring 1 inch of water to a boil in a medium saucepan over high heat. Reduce the heat to low to keep the water at a steady simmer. Choose a heatproof medium bowl that will fit over, but not in, the water in the saucepan (do not allow the bottom of the bowl to touch the water). Whisk the egg yolks and white, Marsala, sugar, and vanilla in the bowl. Set the bowl in the saucepan over the simmering water. Whisk constantly until the mixture warms and is thickened, light, and fluffy, like whipped cream, about 3 minutes.

3. Remove from the heat and immediately spoon equal amounts of the zabaglione over the berries. Serve immediately.

Zucchini Cake

Makes 8 servings

I know I said to avoid cake, but just take a look at the ingredients and you can see this is not one you have to skip. It has none of the evil offenders like vegetable oil (when cooking with just a tablespoon or two, it isn't so bad; it's when you dump cupfuls into a dessert that you should get nervous). Most of the moistness comes from low-fat buttermilk. We call it a "cake," but truth be told, it's more like a dessert bread. With zucchini and walnuts, it packs a pretty healthy punch, and is amazing with your after-dinner espressso.

---

2 ½ cups all-purpose flour, plus more for the pan

1 teaspoon baking soda

1 teaspoon salt

8 tablespoons (1 stick) unsalted butter, at room temperature, plus more for the pan

1¼ cups granulated sugar

2 large eggs

½ cup reduced-fat buttermilk (or use ½ cup reduced-fat milk mixed with 1 tablespoon fresh lemon juice)

1½ cups shredded zucchini (about 2 medium zucchini), shredded on the large holes of a box grater

1 teaspoon vanilla extract

1 cup coarsely chopped walnuts

1. Preheat the oven to 350ºF. Lightly butter the inside of an 8½ x 4½ x 2½-inch loaf pan. Line the bottom of the pan with waxed paper. Dust the sides with flour and tap out the excess.

2. Beat the butter in a medium bowl with an electric mixer on high speed until smooth, about 1 minute. Gradually beat in the sugar and beat until the mixture is very pale (it won't be light and fluffy), about 3 minutes. One at a time, beat in the eggs, beating well after each addition. Reduce the mixer speed to low. In 3 additions, alternating with 2 equal additions of the buttermilk, mix in the flour mixture, scraping down the sides of the bowl with a rubber spatula as needed. Mix in the zucchini and walnuts. Spread the batter evenly in the pan.

3. Bake until the cake is golden brown and a long wooden skewer inserted in the center comes out clean, about 1¼ hours. Let cool in the pan on a wire cooling rack for 10 minutes. Invert the cake onto the rack, remove the waxed paper, turn right-side up, and let cool completely. Cut into slices and serve. (The cake can be stored, wrapped in plastic wrap and refrigerated, for up to 1 week.)

Berry-Ricotta Tiramisù

Makes 4 servings

You didn't think it was possible to do a low-fat tiramisù did you? But it is! Most people make tiramisù with mascarpone, which is just about the richest, most buttery cheese available. You can get the same creamy texture, but not the fat, from low-fat ricotta thinned with a little low-fat milk. For a really nice presentation, make these in individual servings. Parfait glasses look great, but you could also use ramekins, glass custard cups, or even drinking glasses. The idea is to let everyone see the pretty layering.

3/4 cup low-fat ricotta cheese

3 tablespoons low-fat (1%) milk

3 tablespoons confectioners' sugar, divided

1/4 cup cold brewed French or Italian roast coffee

1 tablespoon dark or golden rum

8 savoiardi (dry ladyfingers), crushed into crumbs in a plastic bag with a rolling pin

2/3 cup fresh raspberries (about half of a 6-ounce container)

1/2 ounce (1/2 square) semisweet chocolate

1. Have ready four 4-ounce parfait glasses. You can also use cocktail glasses, custard cups, or ramekins, preferably glass, of about the same capacity.

2. Mash the ricotta, milk, and 2 tablespoons of confectioners' sugar together in a small bowl with a rubber spatula until the mixture is smooth. Mix the coffee, rum, and remaining tablespoon confectioners' sugar together in another small bowl.

3. For each serving, put the equivalent of 1 cookie (about 2 tablespoons of crumbs) in the bottom of a parfait glass. Sprinkle with a scant 2 teaspoons of the coffee mixture. Top with 2 tablespoons of the ricotta mixture. Repeat with the cookie crumbs, coffee mixture, and ricotta mixture. Cover each with plastic wrap and refrigerate until chilled, at least 1 hour and up to 1 day.

4. Just before serving, top each tiramisù with an equal amount of berries. Using the large holes on a box grater, grate the chocolate onto a sheet of waxed paper. Lift up the waxed paper and use it to help sprinkle the chocolate over the berries (if you touch the grated chocolate, it will melt). Serve chilled.

Pignoli Cookies

Makes about 3 dozen cookies

These are my absolute favorite cookies. Come to my house bearing a box of these, and you're a friend forever! *Pignoli* means "pine nut" in Italian. The nuts that the cookies are rolled in make them easy to spot anywhere—but they get the bulk of their flavor from the almond paste. Even though these are cookies (and you should resist eating a whole tray of them!), they don't have any oil, butter, shortening, chocolate, or other diet-busting ingredients. Just one egg white, a little sugar, and delicious, nutritious nuts.

2 (7-ounce) tubes almond paste
1⅓ cups confectioners' sugar
1 large egg white
½ teaspoon vanilla extract
¾ cup (3 ounces) pine nuts

1. Position a rack in the center of the oven and preheat the oven to 350ºF. Line 2 large baking sheets with parchment paper or use nonstick baking sheets.

2. Crumble the almond paste into a large, deep bowl. Sprinkle about half of the confectioners' sugar over the almond paste. Beat with an electric mixer on medium speed, gradually adding the remaining sugar until the mixture is broken into fine crumbs. Add the egg white and vanilla and beat until smooth and the mixture forms a sticky dough. Let stand for 5 minutes.

3. Using a heaping teaspoon for each cookie, roll into 36 balls, each about 1-inch wide. Put the pine nuts in a small bowl. Roll each ball in the pine nuts to coat. Arrange the balls on the baking sheets about 1 inch apart. Using the heel of your hand, slightly press each ball to spread into a round about 2 inches in diameter.

4. Bake the cookies, one sheet at a time (leave the second sheet uncovered and at room temperature while baking the first batch), until the cookies are golden brown, 15 to 18 minutes. Let the cookies cool on the cookie sheet for 3 minutes. Transfer the cookies to wire cooling racks and cool completely. (The cookies can be stored in an airtight container for up to 1 week.)

Apple Crostata

Makes 6 servings

Crostata means "tart" in Italian, and usually any kind of filled pie has at least a full stick of butter in it. Not this one! Only three tablespoons, only five ingredients, and you won't believe how delicious it is! And it might be the most gorgeous dessert ever.

3 tablespoons unsalted butter, melted

2 Ginger Gold or Golden Delicious apples

6 frozen thawed phyllo dough sheets (see Note on page 172)

1 tablespoon freshly squeezed lemon juice

2 tablespoons granulated sugar

1. Position a rack in the center of the oven and preheat to 400ºF. Lightly butter a 9-inch glass pie dish with some of the melted butter.

2. Peel and quarter the apples. Cut out the core from each wedge. Place an apple quarter, cut-side down, on a work surface, and cut into very thin (less than 1/8-inch-thick) slices, keeping the slices together.

3. Lay 2 phyllo sheets, overlapping by about 1 inch, in the pie pan, letting the excess dough hang over the sides. Using a soft-bristled pastry brush, lightly brush and drizzle the phyllo with about 2 teaspoons of melted butter. Repeat twice with the remaining phyllo sheets and 4 more teaspoons of butter.

4. Working quickly so the phyllo doesn't dry out, fan the largest apple slices in concentric circles in the pie pan. Fill the empty space in the center of the circle with the smaller apple slices. Brush the apple slices with the lemon juice and sprinkle with the sugar. Loosely roll the edges of the phyllo up to make a 1-inch-wide border of phyllo around the top rim of the dish—remember, it should look rustic, so don't worry about the phyllo crumbling. Brush the phyllo with some of the remaining melted butter and drizzle the last of the butter over the apple slices.

5. Bake until the apples are tender and the crust is golden brown, about 25 minutes. Let cool in the pan on a wire cooling rack for 10 minutes. Slide the crostata out of the pan onto a serving dish. Cut into wedges and serve warm.

Note: Thaw the phyllo overnight in the refrigerator. If have had trouble with phyllo sheets sticking to each other in the past, you probably let it thaw at room temperature. While working with the phyllo, keep the remaining sheets covered with a damp (not wet!) towel to stay moist. You will have leftover phyllo, so look up another recipe to use it before it goes bad. You can't refreeze it.

✳ ✳ ✳ Amore Ristorante ✳ ✳ ✳

One of the ways people end up sabotaging their good diet intentions is by eating out too much. Once you leave your own kitchen, you lose control over the amount of fat and calories stuffed, brushed, fried, or squirted into your food. Eating at home is a healthier (and much less expensive) option. But it doesn't have to feel like the same-old. Especially for special nights, you can turn your love nest into the world's most romantic restaurant.

Get out the good china (what are you saving it for anyway?). Use actual linen napkins. Dim the lights and dig out the candles; the more the better. Put on some soft music. Dress just as beautifully as if you were going out on the town. I've even written up menus before, and yes, sometimes the attire for my home restaurant was lingerie. Get as creative as you can. Do different themed restaurants. Hire some servers. You might even role play . . . Check, please!

Macedonia di Frutta

Makes 6 servings

Italians love to eat fruit for dessert, but this is no boring fruit salad. It's the "juiced" up version—fruit salad on steroids. It's amazing what a little sugar and lemon juice can do; just be sure to refrigerate this for an hour or two to let the juices mingle. You can really use any fruit you want. Try mixing different kinds—stone (ones with pits), citrus (grapefruit or oranges), tropical (pineapple, mango, or kiwi), and berries. Here's the combo I use the most often because the colors look so pretty together and it's delish!

2 ripe medium peaches or apricots

2 ripe kiwi fruits

2 large navel oranges

1 dry quart strawberries, hulled and quartered

1 tablespoon freshly squeezed lemon juice

2 teaspoons granulated sugar

1 ripe banana, cut into ¼-inch rounds

1. Using a vegetable peeler, remove the skins from the peaches and kiwi. (If you have never done this with peaches before, try it. It is much easier that the usual method of dropping the peaches into hot water, then cold water, then peeling. Using the peeler, work around the peaches in a spiral to remove the peel, and not from top to bottom.) Use your fingers to peel the oranges. Cut the peaches, kiwi, and oranges into bite-sized pieces, discarding the pits. Transfer to a medium bowl.

2. Add the strawberries. Sprinkle with the lemon juice and sugar and mix gently. Cover and refrigerate for at least 1 and up to 6 hours.

3. Just before serving, gently mix in the banana. Serve chilled.

Sweet from the Inside

I get a lot of people wondering how I can be so upbeat all the time, even when things look grim. They ask me if it's just an act or—if they're super direct or drunk—if I'm just too stupid to realize bad things are happening to me. Um, how do I put this kindly? No and no. [Smiling while making obscene gesture under my laptop.] Of course I know when bad things are going on. I'm just like everyone else, and difficult times fall on everyone. I choose to smile anyway. My smile doesn't mean I'm ignoring the issue. It means I'm refusing to let it get me down.

Yes, I've had days when I felt like staying in bed and crying all day. Everyone does. But I don't give in. I get up, I smile, and I work toward what I know will be a better day. I do it for two reasons: my dad taught me to never give up, and I'm now teaching the same lesson to my daughters.

In Italy there's a proverb—*Questo mondo è fatto a scale, chi le scende e chi le sale*—that basically means "the world is a ladder." Sometimes you're going up. Sometimes you're going down. The important thing is, you keep moving! There's a Japanese saying that football coaches like to use over here: "Success is falling down seven times, and getting up eight."

Thinking positively and having a good attitude is so, so, so important. It's not only great for your mood, it can also help correct your situation, set a good example for others, and it's actually good for your health. I may be feisty on TV, but if you really watch, I only react; I'm not an attacker. If you've met me at a book signing or even just in an elevator, if you read my blog (teresagiudice.com) or follow me on Twitter (@Teresa_Giudice), you know that in real life I'm a happy person who loves her life, her family, and her fans!

I cannot thank you all enough for welcoming me into your homes. It has been such an honor to share my family's recipes with you all. Nothing gives me more pleasure or inspiration than hearing your own family stories and seeing photos of your beautiful babies. I have to say, I have the most gorgeous, loving fans in the world. I'm extremely blessed by you all.

And with that, I say *Arrivederci!* In Italian, it's literally a toast of optimism: "Until we see each other again."

Tanti Baci,

Teresa xx

> ### When in Rome . . .
>
> Arrivederci = ah-ree-vah-DARE-chee

Nutritional Information

Chapter 2:
Live It Up–I-Can't-Believe-It's-Not-Fattening Food

Chicken with Bruschetta Topping, page 38

Each serving:

calories 290
carbohydrate . . . . 5 g
fat . . . . 12 g
saturated fat . . . . 2 g
cholesterol . . . . 94 mg
fiber . . . . 1 g
protein . . . . 35 g
sodium . . . . 244 mg

Pasta al Forno, page 41

Each serving:

calories 483
carbohydrate . . . . 61 g
fat . . . . 15 g
saturated fat . . . . 5 g
cholesterol . . . . 16 mg
fiber . . . . 11 g
protein . . . . 22 g
sodium . . . . 810 mg

Chicken Milanese, page 42

Each serving:

calories 504
carbohydrate . . . . 42 g
fat . . . . 17 g
saturated fat . . . . 4 g

cholesterol . . . . 96 mg
fiber . . . . 1 g
protein . . . . 43 g
sodium . . . . 638 mg

Fettuccine alla Carbonara, page 44

Each serving:

calories 443
carbohydrate . . . . 59 g
fat . . . . 14 g
saturated fat . . . . 5 g
cholesterol . . . . 80 mg
fiber . . . . 3 g
protein . . . . 19 g
sodium . . . . 317 mg

Veal Stew Osso Buco-Style, page 47

Each serving:

calories 402
carbohydrate . . . . 11 g
fat . . . . 12 g
saturated fat . . . . 3 g
cholesterol . . . . 215 mg
fiber . . . . 2 g
protein . . . . 51 g
sodium . . . . 1214 mg

Roasted Pork Loin
with Peppercorn Crust, page 48

Each serving:

calories 357
carbohydrate . . . . 20 g

fat . . . . 13 g

saturated fat . . . . 4 g

cholesterol . . . . 90 mg

fiber . . . . 2 g

protein . . . . 36 g

sodium . . . . 540 mg

Chapter 3:
Serve It Up–Amazing Antipasti

Clams Casino, page 52
Each serving:

calories 203

carbohydrate . . . . 12 g

fat . . . . 12 g

saturated fat . . . . 3 g

cholesterol . . . . 25 mg

fiber . . . . 1 g

protein . . . . 11 g

sodium . . . . 543 mg

Ciambotta, page 54
Each serving:

calories 86

carbohydrate . . . . 5 g

fat . . . . 7 g

saturated fat . . . . 1 g

cholesterol . . . . 0 mg

fiber . . . . 2 g

protein . . . . 1 g

sodium . . . . 221 mg

Creamy Tomato and Basil Dip, page 55
Each serving:

calories 49

carbohydrate . . . . 5 g

fat . . . . 1 g

saturated fat . . . . 0 g

cholesterol . . . . 3 mg

fiber . . . . 0 g

protein . . . . 7 g

sodium . . . . 224 mg

Caprese Cherry Tomatoes, page 57
Each serving:

calories 71

carbohydrate . . . . 3 g

fat . . . . 5 g

saturated fat . . . . 4 g

cholesterol . . . . 16 mg

fiber . . . . 1 g

protein . . . . 4 g

sodium . . . . 119 mg

Fruit and Proscuitto Crostini, page 58
Each serving:

calories 112

carbohydrate . . . . 16 g

fat . . . . 3 g

saturated fat . . . . 1 g

cholesterol . . . . 4 mg

fiber . . . . 1 g

protein . . . . 5 g

sodium . . . . 353 mg

Chapter 4:
Soup It Up–Hot & Cold
Comfort Food

Rustic Lentil Soup, page 63
Each serving:

calories 234

carbohydrate . . . . 41 g

fat . . . . 2 g saturated fat . . . . 2 g

cholesterol . . . . O mg

fiber . . . . 11 g

protein . . . . 14 g

sodium . . . . 239 mg

Zuppa di Verdure, page 65

Each serving:

calories 113

carbohydrate . . . . 15 g

fat . . . . 4 g

saturated fat . . . . 1 g

cholesterol . . . . 4 mg

fiber . . . . 2 g

protein . . . . 7 g

sodium . . . . 809 mg

Italian Wedding Soup, page 66

Each serving:

calories 194

carbohydrate . . . . 11 g

fat . . . . 8 g

saturated fat . . . . 3 g

cholesterol . . . . 83 mg

fiber . . . . 2 g

protein . . . . 19 g

sodium . . . . 1136 mg

Chilled Cream of Asparagus Soup, page 69

Each serving:

calories 114

carbohydrate . . . . 9 g

fat . . . . 7 g

saturated fat . . . . 3 g

cholesterol . . . . 18 mg

fiber . . . . 2 g

protein . . . . 6 g

sodium . . . . 588 mg

Calamari and Potato Cacciuco, page 70

Each serving:

calories 193

carbohydrate . . . . 27 g

fat . . . . 3 g

saturated fat . . . . 1 g

cholesterol . . . . 152 mg

fiber . . . . 5 g

protein . . . . 13 g

sodium . . . . 339 mg

Stracciatella with Spinach, page 71

Each serving:

calories 85

carbohydrate . . . . 4 g

fat . . . . 4 g

saturated fat . . . . 2 g

cholesterol . . . . 68 mg

fiber . . . . 1 g

protein . . . . 10 g

sodium . . . . 903 mg

Chapter 5:
Switch It Up—Low-Fat Italian Classics

Skinny Spaghetti Bolognese, page 76

Each serving:

calories 457

carbohydrate . . . . 70 g

fat . . . . 9 g

saturated fat . . . . 1 g

cholesterol . . . . 27 mg

fiber . . . . 11 g

protein . . . . 23 g

sodium . . . . 681 mg

Veal and Peppers, page 77

Each serving:

calories 263
carbohydrate . . . . 12 g
fat . . . . 9 g
saturated fat . . . . 2 g
cholesterol . . . . 129 mg
fiber . . . . 2 g
protein . . . . 32 g
sodium . . . . 716 mg

Turkey Meatballs, page 78

Each serving:

calories 327
carbohydrate . . . . 22 g
fat . . . . 13 g
saturated fat . . . . 3 g
cholesterol . . . . 113 mg
fiber . . . . 3 g
protein . . . . 29 g
sodium . . . . 1155 mg

Lasagna Rustica, page 79

Each serving:

calories 414
carbohydrate . . . . 36 g
fat . . . . 15 g
saturated fat . . . . 5 g
cholesterol . . . . 77 mg
fiber . . . . 5 g
protein . . . . 27 g
sodium . . . . 1341 mg

Faux Fettuccine Alfredo with Broccoli, page 82

Each serving:

calories 428
carbohydrate . . . . 70 g

fat . . . . 9 g
saturated fat . . . . 4 g
cholesterol . . . . 17 mg
fiber . . . . 5 g
protein . . . . 20 g
sodium . . . . 312 mg

Naked Chicken Parmesan, page 85

Each serving:

calories 364
carbohydrate . . . . 10 g
fat . . . . 15 g
saturated fat . . . . 5 g
cholesterol . . . . 106 mg
fiber . . . . 3 g
protein . . . . 42 g
sodium . . . . 925 mg

Chapter 6:
Step It Up—Gourmet Entrées

Shrimp Scampi, page 88

Each serving:

calories 216
carbohydrate . . . . 4 g
fat . . . . 14 g
saturated fat . . . . 6 g
cholesterol . . . . 202 mg
fiber . . . . 0 g
20 g protein . . . .
949 mg sodium . . . .

Veal Scaloppine, page 90

Each serving:

calories 393
carbohydrate . . . . 11 g
fat . . . . 24 g

saturated fat . . . . 7 g

cholesterol . . . . 92 mg

fiber . . . . l g

protein . . . . 27 g

sodium . . . . 434 mg

Tagliatelle alla Boscaiola, page 91

Each serving:

calories 355

carbohydrate . . . . 63 g

fat . . . . 6 g

saturated fat . . . . 2 g

cholesterol . . . . 7 mg

fiber . . . . 4 g

protein . . . . 14 g

sodium . . . . 244 mg

Pollo Involtini, page 93

Each serving:

calories 289

carbohydrate . . . . 6 g

fat . . . . 10 g

saturated fat . . . . 3 g

cholesterol . . . . 100 mg

fiber . . . . 2 g

protein . . . . 38 g

sodium . . . . 578 mg

Herb-Crusted Tilapia, page 94

Each serving:

calories 293

carbohydrate . . . . 12 g

fat . . . . 11 g

saturated fat . . . . 2 g

cholesterol . . . . 85 mg

fiber . . . . O g

protein . . . . 37 g

sodium . . . . 414 mg

Risotto Cacciatore, page 96

Each serving:

calories 350

carbohydrate . . . . 48 g

fat . . . . 9 g

saturated fat . . . . 2 g

cholesterol . . . . 4 mg

fiber . . . . 3 g

protein . . . . 13 g

sodium . . . . 915 mg

Chapter 7:
Grill It Up–Sizzling Selections

Chicken Spiedini, page 101

Each serving:

calories 256

carbohydrate . . . . 12 g

fat . . . . 11 g

saturated fat . . . . 2 g

cholesterol . . . . 65 mg

fiber . . . . l g

protein . . . . 26 g

sodium . . . . 254 mg

Rosemary Shrimp Skewers, page 102

Each serving:

calories 115

carbohydrate . . . . 2 g

fat . . . . 5 g

saturated fat . . . . l g

cholesterol . . . . 143 mg

fiber . . . . O g

protein . . . . 16 g

sodium . . . . 787 mg

Grilled Tuna with Asparagus, page 103

Each serving:

calories 311
carbohydrate . . . . 7 g
fat . . . . 12 g
saturated fat . . . . 2 g
cholesterol . . . . 67 mg
fiber . . . . 2 g
protein . . . . 43 g
sodium . . . . 516 mg

Steak Salad with Light Balsamic Vinaigrette, page 104

Each serving:

346calories . . . .
11 g carbohydrate . . . .
17 g fat . . . .
4 g saturated fat . . . .
91 mg cholesterol . . . .
2 g fiber . . . .
35 g protein . . . .
359 mg sodium . . . .

Zesty Grilled Pork Loin Chops, page 106

Each serving:

calories 283
carbohydrate . . . . 1 g
fat . . . . 16 g
saturated fat . . . . 4 g
cholesterol . . . . 100 mg
fiber . . . . 0 g
protein . . . . 32 g
sodium . . . . 358 mg

Grilled Italian Vegetables, page 107

Each serving:

calories 94
carbohydrate . . . . 7 g

fat . . . . 7 g
saturated fat . . . . 1 g
cholesterol . . . . 0 mg
fiber . . . . 3 g
protein . . . . 2 g
sodium . . . . 151 mg

Veggie-Stuffed Portobello Mushrooms, page 108

Each serving:

calories 188
carbohydrate . . . . 15 g
fat . . . . 11 g
saturated fat . . . . 4 g
cholesterol . . . . 12 mg
fiber . . . . 4 g
protein . . . . 6 g
sodium . . . . 381 mg

Chapter 8:
Veg It Up—Vegetarian Meals & Side Dishes

Asparagus and Potato Frittata, page 114

Each serving:

calories 137
carbohydrate . . . . 8 g
fat . . . . 8 g
saturated fat . . . . 2 g
cholesterol . . . . 125 mg
fiber . . . . 1 g
protein . . . . 8 g
sodium . . . . 291 mg

Balsamic Green Beans, page 116

Each serving:

calories 60
carbohydrate . . . . 6 g
fat . . . . 4 g
saturated fat . . . . 1 g
cholesterol . . . . 0 mg
fiber . . . . 2 g
protein . . . . 1 g
sodium . . . . 151 mg

Roasted Cauliflower with Garlic and Olives, page 117

Each serving:

calories 98
carbohydrate . . . . 7 g
fat . . . . 7 g
saturated fat . . . . 1 g
cholesterol . . . . 3 mg
fiber . . . . 3 g
protein . . . . 4 g
sodium . . . . 351 mg

Easy Risi e Bisi, page 118

Each serving:

calories 251
carbohydrate . . . . 45 g
fat . . . . 4 g
saturated fat . . . . 1 g
cholesterol . . . . 3 mg
fiber . . . . 2 g
protein . . . . 8 g
sodium . . . . 443 mg

Escarole and Beans, page 119

Each serving:

calories 156
carbohydrate . . . . 23 g

fat . . . . 4 g
saturated fat . . . . 1 g
cholesterol . . . . 0 mg
fiber . . . . 9 g
protein . . . . 9 g
sodium . . . . 472 mg

Peperonata, page 121

Each serving:

calories 89
carbohydrate . . . . 14 g
fat . . . . 2 g
saturated fat . . . . 0 g
cholesterol . . . . 0 mg
fiber . . . . 2 g
protein . . . . 2 g
sodium . . . . 86 mg

Piselli al Prosciutto, page 122

Each serving:

calories 95
carbohydrate . . . . 9 g
fat . . . . 4 g
saturated fat . . . . 1 g
cholesterol . . . . 4 mg
fiber . . . . 3 g
protein . . . . 5 g
sodium . . . . 266 mg

Very Veggie Roast, page 123

Each serving:

calories 105
carbohydrate . . . . 11 g
fat . . . . 7 g
saturated fat . . . . 1 g
cholesterol . . . . 0 mg
fiber . . . . 5 g

protein . . . . 3 g

sodium . . . . 203 mg

Chapter 9:
Whip It Up—Extra Fast Food

Italian Chicken Stir Fry, page 128
Each serving:

calories 242

carbohydrate . . . . 9 g

fat . . . . 10 g

saturated fat . . . . 2 g

cholesterol . . . . 67 mg

fiber . . . . 3 g

28 g protein . . . .

520 mg sodium . . . .

Cavatappi Puttanesca, page 129
Each serving:

391 calories . . . .

64 g carbohydrate . . . .

6 g fat . . . .

1 g saturated fat . . . .

15 mg cholesterol . . . .

4 g fiber . . . .

18 g protein . . . .

682 mg sodium . . . .

Gnocchi with Pink Tomato Sauce,
page 130
Each serving:

387 calories . . . .

66 g carbohydrate . . . .

8 g fat . . . .

3 g saturated fat . . . .

17 mg cholesterol . . . .

5 g fiber . . . .

14 g protein . . . .

998 mg sodium . . . .

Lingurian Buridda (Seafood Stew),
page 131
Each serving:

calories 172

carbohydrate . . . . 8 g

fat . . . . 4 g

saturated fat . . . . 1 g

cholesterol . . . . 93 mg

fiber . . . . 2 g

protein . . . . 24 g

sodium . . . . 606 mg

Cappellini with Two-Tomato Sauce
and Basil, page 132
Each serving:

calories 337

carbohydrate . . . . 63 g

fat . . . . 5 g

saturated fat . . . . 1 g

cholesterol . . . . 4 mg

fiber . . . . 11 g

protein . . . . 14 g

sodium . . . . 236 mg

Penne Primavera, page 133
Each serving:

calories 360

carbohydrate . . . . 54 g

fat . . . . 7 g

saturated fat . . . . 4 g

cholesterol . . . . 11 mg

fiber . . . . 10 g

protein . . . . 18 g

sodium . . . . 331 mg

Salmon alla Sala Consilina, page 135

Each serving:

calories 451
carbohydrate .... 5 g
fat .... 30 g
saturated fat .... 6 g
cholesterol .... 94 mg
fiber .... 1 g
protein .... 36 g
sodium .... 573 mg

Shrimp Salad with Diablo Dressing, 142

Each serving:

calories 215
carbohydrate .... 4 g
fat .... 9 g
saturated fat .... 1 g
cholesterol .... 230 mg
fiber .... 1 g
protein .... 29 g
sodium .... 630 mg

Gemelli L'estate, page 136

Each serving:

calories 380
carbohydrate .... 64 g
fat .... 8 g
saturated fat .... 2 g
cholesterol .... 4 mg
fiber .... 5 g
protein .... 14 g
sodium .... 293 mg

Hot Mussels Marinara, 145

Each serving:

calories 229
carbohydrate .... 10 g
fat .... 6 g
saturated fat .... 1 g
cholesterol .... 42 mg
fiber .... 1 g
protein .... 19 g
sodium .... 589 mg

Chapter 10:
Spice It Up–Some Like It HOT

Linguine Indiavolati, page 141

Each serving:

calories 351
carbohydrate .... 65 g
fat .... 4 g
saturated fat .... 1 g
cholesterol .... 9 mg
fiber .... 11 g
protein .... 18 g
sodium .... 599 mg

Spicy Pork Choplets, page 146

Each serving:

calories 325
carbohydrate .... 5 g
fat .... 16 g
saturated fat .... 4 g
cholesterol .... 90 mg
fiber .... 1 g
protein .... 35 g
sodium .... 568 mg

Spaghettini alla Carrettiera, page 147

Each serving:

calories 372
carbohydrate . . . . 64 g
fat . . . . 8 g
saturated fat . . . . 2 g
cholesterol . . . . 4 mg
fiber . . . . 11 g
protein . . . . 15 g
sodium . . . . 364 mg

Chapter 11:
Sex It Up—Romantic Meals

Sexy Chickpea Chard Stew, page 152

Each serving:

calories 204
carbohydrate . . . . 33 g
fat . . . . 5 g
saturated fat . . . . 1 g
cholesterol . . . . 0 mg
fiber . . . . 8 g
protein . . . . 10 g
sodium . . . . 1232 mg

Chicken di Firenze, page 153

Each serving:

calories 302
carbohydrate . . . . 14 g
fat . . . . 13 g
saturated fat . . . . 3 g
cholesterol . . . . 77 mg
fiber . . . . 4 g
protein . . . . 35 g
sodium . . . . 686 mg

Heavenly Halibut, page 155

Each serving:

calories 379
carbohydrate . . . . 1 g
fat . . . . 28 g
saturated fat . . . . 5 g
cholesterol . . . . 84 mg
fiber . . . . 0 g
protein . . . . 27 g
sodium . . . . 473 mg

Italian Flank Steak with Smothered Onions, page 156

Each serving:

calories 375
carbohydrate . . . . 19 g
fat . . . . 18 g
saturated fat . . . . 6 g
cholesterol . . . . 71 mg
fiber . . . . 3 g
protein . . . . 30 g
sodium . . . . 505 mg

Red Snapper with Herbed Tomato Sauce, page 157

Each serving:

calories 286
carbohydrate . . . . 12 g
fat . . . . 9 g
saturated fat . . . . 1 g
cholesterol . . . . 60 mg
fiber . . . . 2 g
protein . . . . 36 g
sodium . . . . 808 mg

Pesce all' Acqua Pazza, page 158

Each serving:

calories 253
carbohydrate . . . . 6 g
fat . . . . 7 g
saturated fat . . . . 1 g
cholesterol . . . . 74 mg
fiber . . . . 1 g
protein . . . . 34 g
sodium . . . . 273 mg

Zucchini Cake, page 165

Each serving:

calories 505
carbohydrate . . . . 66 g
fat . . . . 24 g
saturated fat . . . . 9 g
cholesterol . . . . 81 mg
fiber . . . . 2 g
protein . . . . 9 g
sodium . . . . 490 mg

Chapter 12:
Sweeten It Up—
Guilt-Free Desserts

Espresso Granita, page 163

Each serving:

calories 95
carbohydrate . . . . 24 g
fat . . . . 0 g
saturated fat . . . . 0 g
cholesterol . . . . 0 mg
fiber . . . . 0 g
protein . . . . 0 g
sodium . . . . 10 mg

Berry-Ricotta Tiramisù, page 167

Each serving:

calories 211
carbohydrate . . . . 26 g
fat . . . . 7 g
saturated fat . . . . 4 g
cholesterol . . . . 64 mg
fiber . . . . 2 g
protein . . . . 9 g
sodium . . . . 96 mg

Mixed Berry Zabaglione, 164

Each serving:

calories 129
carbohydrate . . . . 19 g
fat . . . . 3 g
saturated fat . . . . 1 g
cholesterol . . . . 123 mg
fiber . . . . 4 g
protein . . . . 3 g
sodium . . . . 17 mg

Pignoli Cookies, page 168

Each serving (2 cookies):

calories 170
carbohydrate . . . . 20 g
fat . . . . 9 g
saturated fat . . . . 1 g
cholesterol . . . . 0 mg
fiber . . . . 1 g
protein . . . . 3 g
sodium . . . . 8 mg

Apple Crostata, page 171

Each serving:

calories 156
carbohydrate . . . . 23 g
fat . . . . 7 g

saturated fat . . . . 4 g

cholesterol . . . . 15 mg

fiber . . . . 2 g

protein . . . . 2 g

sodium . . . . 93 mg

Macedonia di Frutta, page 173

Each serving:

calories 114

carbohydrate . . . . 28 g

fat . . . . 1 g

saturated fat . . . . 0 g

cholesterol . . . . 0 mg

fiber . . . . 5 g

protein . . . . 2 g

sodium . . . . 2 mg

Index

5/14 bm